THE TRINITARIAN
CONTROVERSY

THE TRINITARIAN CONTROVERSY

Translated and Edited by William G. Rusch

Supplemental Material by Robert C. Saler

Fortress Press

Minneapolis

THE TRINITARIAN CONTROVERSY
Translated and Edited by William G. Rusch

ISBN: 978-0-8006-1410-2

Library of Congress Cataloging in Publication Data
The Trinitarian controversy.
(Sources of early Christian thought)
Bibliography: p.
Trinity—History of doctrines—Early church, ca. 30-600. 2. Trinity—Early works to 1800. I. Rusch, William G. II. Series.
BT109.T74   231'044
ISBN 0-8006-1410-0

Contents

1

Introduction

This volume is a collection of primary texts illustrating the most crucial phase of that lengthy process by which the early Christians reached a coherent doctrine of God. The period under discussion, generally known as the trinitarian controversy, dates from around A.D. 319, the preaching of Arius, to about A.D. 419, the completion of Augustine's *On the Trinity*, although the main features of the resolution of this dispute were set by A.D. 381 with the Council of Constantinople. In the sources presented here, there can be observed an interplay of various theological understandings, as well as of personalities and politics. The Christian community did not formulate its doctrine of God as a purely theological exercise, divorced from other pressures. Nontheological factors played a significant, although in the final analysis, minor role. These documents reveal that essentially a theological process is unfolding. The church in this discussion was seeking to distinguish its faith from paganism and to affirm the salvific character of its message.

To understand what is depicted in these texts, the reader must be aware that the commencement of Christian deliberation about God predates by some two centuries the matters which reached their climax in the fourth and fifth centuries. The intention of this introduction is therefore twofold: (1) to narrate, in general terms, the significant developments prior to the year 300, and (2) to provide a context for the documents in this volume, so that they may be allowed to speak for themselves with greater clarity.

Through all the turmoil and tomes, there is one basic issue at the center of the debate: What is the relation of the divine in Christ to the divine in the Father? Or, to put the matter somewhat differently, how is the church, in an intellectually satisfying manner, to integrate the doctrine of one God, Father and Creator, inherited from the Old Testament and Judaism, with the revelation that this God had disclosed himself uniquely in Jesus and had given the Holy Spirit to the church? It will become readily apparent that there were no quick or easily accessible answers that protected both aspects of the tension: the monotheism so deeply ingrained in the biblical tradition, and the distinctiveness and divinity of the Son.

THE BIBLICAL BACKGROUND

From the Old Testament and the Judaism of the intertestamental period, the early church accepted the conviction that God, the maker of heaven and earth, is one. On occasion it supported this teaching with reference to the Stoicism of its day, a philosophy heavily influenced by Platonism, but the dominant influence was clearly the monotheistic faith unfolded within the Old Testament and Judaism. In addition, even before the canonization of the New Testament books, the apostolic traditions and popular faith of the church were indelibly marked by the notion of a plurality of divine persons. The early catechetical and liturgical formulas refer to the Father and the Lord Jesus Christ, or to the Father the Creator, his Son Jesus Christ, and the Holy Spirit.

These twofold and threefold patterns are evident within the New Testament itself. The binitarian formulas are found in Rom. 8:11, 2 Cor. 4:14, Gal. 1:1, Eph. 1:20, 1 Tim. 1:2, 1 Pet. 1:21, and 2 John 1:13. The triadic schema is discovered in Matt. 28:19, 1 Cor. 6:11 and 12:4ff., Gal. 3:11-14, Heb. 10:29, and 1 Pet. 1:2. All these passages indicate that there is no fixity of wording. No doctrine of the Trinity in the Nicene sense is present in the New Testament. However, the threefold pattern is evident throughout, in spite of the fact that there is usually nothing in the context to demand it. The conclusion seems obvious: the idea of the triadic manifestation of the Godhead was present from the earliest period as part of Christian piety and thinking. But no steps were taken to work through the implications of this idea and to arrive at a cohesive doctrine of God. The triadic pattern supplies the raw data from which the more developed descriptions of the Christian doctrine of God will come.

THE SECOND CENTURY

The Apostolic Fathers

Immediately following the New Testament, and indeed overlapping in time with some of the latest books in the New Testament, is a number of writings known collectively as "the Apostolic Fathers." The collection includes writings of Clement of Rome, Ignatius of Antioch, Hermas, Polycarp, and Papias and the *Letter of Barnabas*, the *Letter to Diognetus*, *2 Clement*, and the *Didache*. These works do not offer any systematic theology. They are occasional pieces, called forth by contemporary needs, which tend, often in a pedestrian way, to witness to the traditional ideas and language of the churches rather than to attempt to understand the faith. There are passages in this collection that reflect the view of one God, the Creator (*1 Clement 8, 19, 20; Didache 10; Shepherd of Hermas, Visions 1.1.3*). The question of the relation of the Father and the Son is not addressed, but there is evidence of the triadic schema (*1 Clem.* 46 and 58; Ignatius's *Letter to the Magnesians* 13, the *Letter to the Ephesians* 9). Christ is often called "our God," and prayer to Christ is assumed (Ignatius *Eph.* 18, 20). The Spirit is regarded as inspiring the prophets (*1 Clem.* 8, 13, 16; *Barn.* 6.14; 12.2). Christ's preexistence and role in creation and redemption are assumed (*2 Clem.* 3, 9). His divine element is understood often to be preexistent spirit, and there were even attempts to interpret Christ as a supreme angel (*Shepherd of Hermas, Similitudes* 8.3.3 and 9.1.1). There is no doctrine of the Trinity in the strict sense in the Apostolic Fathers, but the trinitarian formulas are apparent. The witness of this collection of writings to a Christian doctrine of God is slight and provides no advance in synthesis or theological construction beyond the biblical materials.

The Apologists

This is not the case with the works of the Apologists of the second century, Aristides, Justin Martyr, Athenagoras, Tatian, and Theophilus of Antioch. Although they differ among themselves in several aspects, these authors shared a common concern to present Christianity to the Greco-Roman culture of their day in such a way as to defend Christianity against the charge of atheism. To the educated classes of the Greco-Roman world, they insisted that the truth of Christianity is that to which the pagan philosophers pointed. In order to substantiate this viewpoint, they employed the concept of the Logos (Word), already known to Judaism and Stoicism. A special debt was owed to the Jewish philosopher Philo of Alexandria, who taught that the divine Logos had spoken through the prophets and had been the subject of the theophanies of the Old Testament. This Logos also is the reason in which all human beings take part. The Greek word *logos*, which means both "word" and "reason" (rationality), allowed this double sense. According to the Apologists, Christ is the Logos, preexistent before the incarnation as the Father's mind or thought. In Christ the Logos became incarnate, but the incarnation was not the beginning of his being. As revealed in creation and redemption, Christ is the Father's expression or extrapolation. By this concept the Apologists were able to maintain both the pretemporal unity of Christ with the Father, and the Son's manifestation in time and space. They found the Stoic distinction between the *Logos endiathetos* (the immanent Word) and the *Logos prophorikos* (the expressed Word) helpful in this regard and even used this terminology. (For example, Theophilus, who was bishop of Antioch in the late second century, employed it in his *Apology to Autolycus* 22).

However, it is in the works of Justin Martyr, a pagan philosopher who converted to Christianity about A.D. 130 and was martyred about 165, that this approach is readily observable. Justin began with the idea of the *Logos spermatikos* (the seminal Word) planted in all persons incompletely and in a fragmentary manner. Before Christ, human beings had "seeds" of the Word and could reach only fragments of the truth (*1 Apology 32.8; 2 Apology 8.1;*

10.2). It is the Logos, Christ himself incarnate, who reveals the source and ground of these fragments of truth (2 *Apol.* 10.1). This Logos was distinct from the Father not only in name but also in number (*Dialogue with Trypho* 128.4). The Logos put forth as the offspring of the Father was with him before all creatures (*Trypho* 62.4). He is divine and God (1 *Apol.* 63.15; *Trypho* 63.5). This identification of Christ with the Logos allowed the Apologists to insist that Christianity was faith in him to whom the Old Testament witnessed and to whom the pagan philosophers indistinctly pointed. It also offered an explanation of how God, unoriginate, eternal, and nameless, could be involved in a changeable world. For Justin, in addition to the incarnation, the Logos functioned as the Father's agent in creation and in revealing truth (1 *Apol.* 59; 64.5; 5.4; 46).

The immanent Word became the expressed Word by the act of generation or putting forth. The Apologists tried to explain this generation by the analogy of the utterance of human speech or of kindling one fire from another fire (Justin, *Trypho* 61.2; 128.3). These ideas reoccur in Tatian, a native of Assyria and a student of philosophy, who had studied with Justin (*Oration to the Greeks* 5.1); in Athenagoras, a Christian philosopher in Athens (*Supplication to Marcus Aurelius* 10.1ff.); and in Theophilus of Antioch (*Autol.* 2.10; 2.22). Thus the Logos concept enabled the Apologists to make clear the distinction between the Logos and the Father.

The Apologists were also cautious lest the monotheism of the church's faith be destroyed. All were concerned to explain that the expression of the Logos did not mean that the Father was deprived of his Word, nor did it involve a partition of the divine substance. To emphasize the essential identity of the Logos with the Father, they used the biblical image of Son or Child for the Logos, so they spoke of the Logos not as a creature but as the offspring by generation (Justin *Trypho* 62.105, 125; 1 *Apol.* 21). They considered the Logos' eligibility for the title "Son" to date from his expression from the Godhead not from his origination with the Father. They also regarded the term "Father" not a title for the first person, as would be the case in later theologians, but for the one Godhead, the author of whatever existed.

Although the Apologists had less to say about the Holy Spirit, they do bear witness to the threefold pattern. Justin coordinates the three persons referring to materials dealing with baptism and the eucharist (1 *Apol.* 61.3-12). For Athenagoras, the Spirit is the inspirer of the prophets (*Supplic,* 7.2). According to Theophilus, the Spirit is identified with Wisdom (*Autol.* 1.7). Such references reveal that the major concern of the Apologists was with the relationship of Christ and the Father and that little attention was given to the place of the Spirit. Tatian (*Or.* 7.13) does not clearly distinguish the Spirit from the Logos. The Apologists' difficulties about the third entity of the Godhead were compounded by the confusion with the Stoic idea of a wholly immanent spirit within creation and the continuing use of "spirit" as a synonym for "deity" (Athengoras *Supplic.* 16; Tatian *Or.* 4; Theophilus *Autol.* 2.10).

The works of the Apologists divulge the lack of a technical vocabulary sufficient to describe the eternal plurality within the Godhead. Nevertheless, these authors did apprehend the distinctions. To judge the Apologists by post-Nicene theology would be grossly unfair. Isolated passages could be cited to support the notion that the Apologists taught subordination within the deity or that they failed to recognize the preexistence of Christ before his generation, but their total teaching rejects such opinions. The Apologists utilized a picture of a man putting forth his thought and spirit in external activity. This representation allowed them to recognize, although dimly, the eternal plurality in the Godhead and to show how the Word and the Spirit, truly manifested in space and time, could also be within the being of the Father. Their work was a decided contribution to theology, maintaining both the necessary distinction of the plurality and the unity. The Apologists set the future course for trinitarian theology and enabled Christianity to take seriously the presuppositions of Greek philosophy.

Irenaeus of Lyon

Irenaeus from Smyrna studied at Rome and became bishop of Lyon near the end of the second century. His theology formed a bridge between Eastern and Western churches. Building on the accomplishments of the Apologists, Irenaeus reaches a high point in theological reflection in the second century. Irenaeus's trinitarian thought is beholden to his doctrine of creation. God alone, the only Lord, Creator and Father, contained all things and caused them to exist *(Against Heresies* 2.1.1). God is uncreated, ingenerate, the first cause. Irenaeus reconciles his teaching of creation and divine transcendence with the notion of divine immanence in the world by means of the Apologists' teaching of a Logos theology. There are, however, some differences. Even before the expression of the Logos from the Godhead, Irenaeus describes him as the Son. He did not wish to be understood as teaching that the Logos became the Son of God because of the incarnation *(Her.* 3.17.4). This view may indicate a certain discomfort with the Apologists' teaching of the two-stage concept of the Logos. Irenaeus tended to approach God in two ways: (1) as he exists in his intrinsic being; (2) as he manifests himself in the "economy," the ordered process of his self-disclosure. Irenaeus prefers the idea of the Logos or Son both eternally with God and expressed *(Her.* 2.30.9; 4.20.3), rather than the Apologists' statement of God's immanent Word coming forth. He refuses to explore the means by which the Word is extrapolated, and he shows a clear dislike for the analogy of human speech as employed by the Apologists. For Irenaeus, God in his inner being is ineffably one, although containing from eternity his Word and Wisdom. In his economy God extrapolates the Son and the Spirit. Irenaeus links the Logos and Spirit in the creative process and speaks of them as God's hands *(Her.* 4.20.2ff.; 5.1.3). The Logos in the flesh displayed the true image of God, but it is the Spirit who makes it possible to receive this revelation, *(Demonstration of the Apostolic Preaching* 7). For Irenaeus the Son is fully divine *(Dem.* 7), as is the Spirit *(Her.* 5.12.2). Thus Irenaeus progressed beyond the Apologists in a fuller recognition of the place of the Spirit and in his idea of economy. Still he is clearly a second-century theologian, as his picture of the Trinity discloses. There is a single personage, the Father, the Godhead itself, with his Word (reason) and his Wisdom. Not only is monotheism reaffirmed, but the real, eternal distinctions in the Godhead are stressed. Irenaeus does this by means of the idea of the economy, the ordered process of the self-disclosure of these distinctions. These distinctions, according to Irenaeus, are only completely revealed in the economy. Nevertheless, they are there from all eternity. Irenaeus's great insight was the use of this imagery to show how the Son and the Spirit disclosed in the economy as other than the Father were also one with him in his intrinsic being. This means of describing the Trinity became known as economic trinitarianism. It was to find both supporters and detractors in the third century.

THE THIRD CENTURY
Monarchianism

During the third century a backlash against the Logos doctrine occurred in the Western church. It was a movement based largely on a fear that the Logos theology endangered the unity of God. Because this reaction wished to accentuate that God was an absolute monad without distinctions within the unity, it became known as monarchianism. Modern handbooks on early Christian doctrine tend to speak of both a modalist monarchianism and a dynamic monarchianism, but among the church fathers "monarchianism" as a term was applied only to the former.

Dynamic monarchianism is another expression for adoptionism, the view that Christ was a mere man upon whom the Spirit descended. Thus, although it was a christological deviation, it was motivated by a concern for divine unity. A number of names are associated with this type of theology. Individuals who lived in Rome in the second and third centuries, Theodotus, Asclepiodotus, and Artemas (or Artemon). More important is Paul of Samosata, bishop of Antioch, who was condemned at a synod in that city in 268. It is difficult to arrive at an accurate picture of what Paul taught. He probably held to a strict unitarian view of God, believing that Son and Spirit were merely names for the inspired person Jesus Christ and the grace given to the apostles. There are similarities between Paul's teaching and economic trinitarianism. Yet his starting point was not the unfolding of an eternal Trinity. It appears that for Paul the Logos is an impersonal communication from God, without individual subsistence so that God is one person, and the threefold distinctions refer only to abstractions except as they are used as traditional terms as Son and Spirit with reference to the man Jesus and the grace of God in the church. A possible source for Paul's thought is the sixth-century work, *De Sectis* 3.3, probably not written by Leontius of Byzantium, an antiMonophysite theologian.

In spite of its similar aim, to safeguard the unity of the Godhead against the teaching of two Gods, modalist monarchianism is quite different. At its simplest, it is the teaching that there is one Godhead which could be designated indifferently as either the Father or the Son. These terms did not indicate any essential distinctions; they were names to be applied to God at different times. God was a monad. There were no numerical distinctions within the monad. This position was taught by Noetus of Smyrna, who lived in Rome at the end of the second century. The sources for this information are Hippolytus, who set himself up in Rome as an antipope in the early third century (in his *Against Noetus*); and Epiphanius, the fourth-century bishop of Salamis (in his the *Refutation of All Heresies*, esp. chap. 57). Noetus may have been identical with a certain Praxeas, against whom Tertullian wrote *(Against Praxeas* 5).

On a more astute and philosophical level, this form of monarchianism was expounded by Sabellius, who was in Rome during the early years of the third century. Sabellianism taught that God was a monad, expressing itself in three operations. Apparently, the Father projected himself first as Son and then as Spirit (Epiphanius *Ref* 62.1.4ff.). This teaching suggests that Sabellius realized some of the problems of the modalism of Noetus and his disciples, and attempted to use features of economic trinitarianism to correct these difficulties. Unfortunately, there is considerable uncertainty in these matters. Most of the evidence comes from over a century after Sabellius and is often confused with the views of Marcellus of Ancyra, a fourth-century writer.

Hippolytus and Tertullian

The trinitarian teaching of Hippolytus and Tertullian can be comprehended only against the backdrop of the rise of monarchianism. Tertullian, who has been described as the father of Latin theology, was born in Carthage. He authored a long list of polemical works and ended his life as a member of the Montanist sect. Ostensibly he was hostile to Greek philosophy, but in fact he was greatly influenced by it, especially by Stoicism. Despite his view of authority as that handed down by the apostles in the rule of faith, his flexibility in treating that tradition allowed him to come to terms with the contributions of the Apologists. Over against certain dualistic views of his day, Tertullian asserted that God the Creator is one *(The Testimony of the Soul* 1; 2). But he refused to understand this in such a way as to be compatible with monarchianism. God did exist in unique solitariness eternally. Nevertheless, he had immanently his Word or reason. Here the analogy of the Apologists is utilized. Both Hippolytus and Tertullian used this image *(Noet.* 10; *Prax.* 5). Tertullian sharpens the individuality of the Word more than his predecessors. The Word is *alius (Prax.* 5). Like the Apologists, Hippolytus and Tertullian teach that the threefoldness of God's intrinsic being is disclosed in creation and redemption *(Noet.* 7.10.14 and *Prax.* 2). Tertullian is actually the first to introduce the Latin *trinitas* into Christian literature. The three are numerically distinct. To explain their roles he uses the Greek term *economy.* What he means by the word is not always clear. Apparently Tertullian means by the term that God's unity is subject to the disposition of the single Godhead into the Father and Son and Spirit to create and redeem. The Word is a person *(persona)* by which he means the concrete presentation of an individual, a second addition to the Father *(Prax.* 7). The Spirit is the representation of the Son *(The Prescription of Heretics* 13). Tertullian took an important step in recognizing the trinitarian distinction of the three persons. In so doing, he also made a special effort to maintain God's essential unity. The threeness of the economy is not incompatible with the unity. The distinction between the three does not involve division or separation. Images of root and its shoot, source, and river are employed *(Apology* 21.11-13; *Prax.* 8). Tertullian states that the Father, Son, and Spirit are one in substance *(Apol.* 21.12; *Prax.* 25). Threeness involves only grade or aspect of these persons of one substance. Tertullian's clear distinction between the three that are of one substance will be an important element in the Nicene formulation.

Hippolytus's ideas are similar but less fully worked out. He too speaks of one God, yet two persons by economy, and third the grace of the Holy Spirit *(Noet.* 14). The need for the threefold structure presents him with difficulties. He is hard-pressed to speak convincingly of the role of the Spirit. For Hippolytus the prominence of the Holy Spirit in the liturgical setting of baptism is acknowledged, but intellectually it is beyond his ability to explain it. Some difference exists between Hippolytus and Tertullian over the use of the title Son. For Hippolytus, the sonship of the Logos begins with the incarnation; for Tertullian, it begins with the Logos' primal generation for creation *(Noet.* 15; *Prax.* 7).

Both Hippolytus and Tertullian then followed in the directions set by the Apologists and Irenaeus in teaching that the three disclosed in the economy are manifestations of a plurality comprehended somewhat obscurely in the inner being of the Godhead. They moved beyond their predecessors in their attempts to indicate the oneness of the substance of which the three were aspects, and in their recognition of the three as persons when revealed in the economy.

Novatian

During this time the theology of the church of Rome tended to be conservative and monarchian in character. Popes like Zephyrinus and Callistus in the early third century were suspicious of the Logos doctrine and of references to distinctions within the Godhead. A more sophisticated theology was developed in Rome by the presbyter Novatian, who became a rigorist and was consecrated an antipope in the year 251. Novatian's thinking showed similarities with Tertullian's, although it contained some older features. In his major writing Novatian declared the Father to be the one Godhead who through his will generated a Son, his Word. This Word existed substantially before creation *(On the Trinity* 16; 31). Novatian defined their relationship in terms of moral unity. He preserves monotheism by speaking of the priority arising from the derivation of the Son. By being begotten, the Son is God, but the derivation shows there is but one God. Here is more than a hint of subordinationism. Novatian also speaks about the deity bestowed by the Father on the Son ever reverting to the Father, and the divine attributes belonging exclusively to the Son *(On Trin.* 31). This teaching implies a mutual interpenetration. In the final analysis, Novatian avoids the notion of two Gods by subordinating the Son to the Father or by making the Son a moment in the divine life of the Father. Little mention is made of the Holy Spirit. The treatment of the Spirit is rudimentary, a description of the work of the Holy Spirit in prophecy, baptism, and sanctification *(On Trin.* 29). The implication is made that the Holy Spirit is a creature *(On Trin.* 7; 8). Novatian's work represents a regression from the levels reached by the Apologists, Irenaeus, and Tertullian.

Clement of Alexandria

Developments of another sort were taking place simultaneously in the Eastern church, around the city of Alexandria, a leading center for the study of Platonism. Clement of Alexandria is one of the important figures involved in these events. Clement was head of the catechetical school at Alexandria around the year 200. He recognized the truth of Greek philosophy but also its partial character. Clement taught that God is transcendent, ineffable, and incomprehensible. He is a unity beyond unity and a monad embracing all reality *(The Tutor* 1.71; *The Stromata* 2.6.1; 5.65.2; 5.78.3; 5.81.3). This is the God who can only be known through his Word or Son. The Son is the image of the Father, his mind or rationality. He is the mediator between the utterly transcendent God, the One, and the world which he contains *(The Exhortation to the Greeks* 98.3; *Strom.* 5.16.3). This Word, both a unity and a plurality, contains the Father's ideas and the forces by which the Father animates the world *(Strom.* 4.156.1ff.). The generation of the Word from the Father is without beginning. The Word is essentially one with him *(Strom.* 4.162.5; 7.22; *Tutor* 1.62.4; 3.101.1). Clement speaks of the Spirit as the light from the Word enlightens the faith. The Spirit is also the power of the Word, which pervades creation and attracts individuals to God *(Strom.* 6.138.1ff.; 7.9.4). Clement presents in a Platonic framework an image of the Trinity which he linked with the Christian triad of Father, Son, and Holy Spirit *(Who Is the Rich Man That Is Saved?* 34.1). Understandably, Clement's trinity, although Christian in character, has a strong resemblance to the triad of Neoplatonism, the One, Mind and World Soul.

Origen

Origen in the first quarter of the third century succeeded Clement as the head of the catechetical school at Alexandria. This voluminous author, biblical scholar, and theologian moved beyond Clement in constructing a theological system that weds the church's threefold understanding of God to the categories of Middle Platonism. Origen's imaginative work represents one of the most significant episodes in the history of theology. Those who succeeded him might oppose his teaching; they were unable to ignore it. Origen began by acknowledging that God is incomprehensible, transcending being itself. God is alone and ingenerate *(First Principles* 1.1.5; 6). God is thus known only indirectly at best, by inference from the universe and the created order. God being perfect brought into existence a world of spiritual beings, souls, co-eternal with himself. Origen believes that God must always have a universe related to him, but the universe is not regarded as a second uncreated principle alongside God *(Princ.* 1.2.10; 2.9.1). It is to mediate between the unity of God and the plurality of spiritual beings that God has his Son, his express image, the meeting place of the plurality *(Against Celsus* 2.64). The relationship between God, the Father, and his Son, the Word (Logos), is eternal. Unlike the Apologists, with their distinction between the immanent Word and the expressed Word, Origen teaches that the "external" expressed relationship is without beginning. The Word's generation is eternal *(Princ.* 1.2.4). It cannot be said that "there was once when he was not," a phrase around which much debate will focus in the next century. This generation cannot be compared with any corporeal process. It is like the emergence of will from mind *(Princ.* 1.2.6). It is an act of the Father's will, a continuous exercise of will, not a single act for economy. Origen's conception of the generation of the Logos is one place where he parted company with philosophy. In Plotinus's thought, the Neoplatonist of the third century, the Mind is not generated by the purposeful will of the One.

The unity between the Father and the Word is described in various ways: in terms of operation, a reflection of a mirror, through the analogy of the union of husband and wife *(Princ.* 1.2.6; *Discussion with Heraclides* 3). Origen realized the importance of the oneness of the Son with the Father. He wished to avoid both monarchianism and the risk of denying Christ's divinity. Origen presented the union as one of love and action. He may also have described it as a substantial union, using the word *homoousios*, but this is not clear *(Fragments on the Epistle to the Hebrews* in *Patrologia Graeca* 14.1308).

At the same time, Origen wished to indicate the distinction between the Father and the Word. He insists that the Son is other in subsistence than the Father. They are two things in respect to persons *(On Prayer* 15.1; *Cel.* 8.12). The Father and Son differ from each other in *hypostasis (The Commentary on the Gospel of St. John* 2.2.10). Originally *hypostasis* and *ousia* were synonyms, the former Stoic and the latter Platonic, meaning real existence or essence. Although *hypostasis* has this original sense in Origen, it is often used in the sense of individual subsistence. The Father is absolutely God, in Greek *the* God, the Word is not. Thus, when the Word is addressed by the title "God" it is *theos* and not *ho theos*. Origen even speaks of the Word as a second God to stress the distinction *(Cel.* 5.39). The Son is the first of Gods; he is the archetype and model. His deity is derived from the fountainhead, the Father. The Word is the archetype because he is always with the Father *(Com. on John* 2.2.10). Thus Origen understands that the Word is God by derivation. In spite of the fact that the Word is one with the Father, he stands on a lower level in the hierarchy. As a mediator between the Father, the Word reflects him to the rational or spiritual creatures who obtain their relation to God through the Word. Here Origen is directly indebted to the Platonism of his day, especially for the view of the need for co-eternal spiritual beings *(logikoi,* whose relation to the Word parallels at a higher level the Word's relation to the Father). Origen, again in the Platonist tradition, sees the Word's derivation of deity from the Father as a continual process of contemplation. Such statements show how Origen thinks of God as being eternally broadened downward by a number of relationships from the fountainhead, the Father, to rational creatures. In this scheme the Word is the mediator between the Father and many rational creatures, which are called by Origen both *logikoi* and *theoi*. Once more, Origen is drawing upon Platonic and Philonic philosophy.

Origen also speaks of the Holy Spirit in the triadic Godhead. The Holy Spirit is not a force or energy of God. He is an active, personal substance *(Fragment 37 on the Gospel of St. John)*. Origen describes the Spirit as chief in rank of all things originated by the Father through Christ *(Com. on John* 2.10.75). This suggests that Origen's Trinity is conceived hierarchically. The Father's action extends to the whole universe, the Son's is restricted to rational creation, the Spirit's to those who are holy *(Princ.* 1.3.5-8). Yet Origen acknowledged that the Spirit operated in creation. The Spirit knows the Father and is one of the Trinity *(Princ.* 1.1.1-5).

It is not accurate to conclude that Origen teaches a triad of disparate beings rather than a trinity. When his Platonic background is noted, it is possible to see how he is holding to a genuine trinitarianism, although with a strongly pluralistic strain. In the final analysis, Origen's use of philosophy was always controlled by his Christian faith. Origen's greatest contribution—and here he decidedly moved beyond all his predecessors—was the teaching that the three (Father, Son and Holy Spirit) are of the eternal mode of God's being and not just determined or evoked by the needs of the economy.

Origen's insight into the Christian understanding of God was of such a caliber that it was to have a lasting impact. But his theological construct was so vast and variegated that his successors often fell into the trap of emphasizing one element of his thought at the expense of other portions, and so failed to keep the required tension that Origen himself had been able to maintain. Therefore, some theologians gave prominence to Origen's insistence on the Son's essential kinship to the Father, for example, Theognostus, head of the catechetical school at Alexandria in the middle of the third century. Others, like Dionysius, bishop of Alexandria, accented Origen's subordinationist strand. Dionysius was accused of sharply separating the Father and the Son, denying the eternity of the Son and declaring him to be a creature of a different substance from the Father. Because of these charges, Dionysius of Alexandria entered into correspondence with the Roman pope, also named Dionysius.

This series of letters clearly illustrates the differing ways in which Western and Eastern theology was developing. Some difference was occasioned by the use of two different languages, Latin and Greek. For example, there was misunderstanding over *hypostasis* and its etymological equivalent *substantia.* But the accents of Western and Eastern theology were caused by more than language. Western theology had for some time been characterized by a monarchian bent. Western theologians put emphasis on the divine unity. Though convinced of the reality of the distinctions within the unity, they had difficulty expressing them apart from the economy. Eastern theologians, much more than their Western counterparts, worked in an atmosphere of Neoplatonism, and so with this legacy developed an approach to the Godhead that, although it recognized the unity, highlighted the distinctions within the unity. Ultimately the issue was two differing approaches to the Christian doctrine of God. These alternate theological perceptions would be evident later in heated contention over the nature of the Christian Trinity.

Before the second half of this introduction, it is useful to summarize this survey. In retrospect it becomes patent that intense deliberation took place among Christians prior to the year 300 about their God. Some explanation of this can be found in the pressure of heretical movements, which aroused Irenaeus and Tertullian to write. The Apologists, Clement, and Origen desired to explain Christianity to their pagan neighbors to prove that it was intellectually respectable and not injurious to the Roman Empire. The curiosity of the early Christians must also be noted. They had an inclination, quite apart from heretical or secular pressures, to probe the implications of their own faith and to articulate it in as cogent a manner as possible. Thus, when the trinitarian controversy arose in the opening years of the fourth century, Christians had a heritage and an arsenal from which to draw. Indeed, in a real sense it is the previous developments outlined above, with their innate tensions, that inevitably led to the outbreak of a dispute that threatened the very existence of the uniqueness of the Christian faith.

THE FOURTH CENTURY

Arius

The central figure of the controversy which so marks the fourth century was Arius, a presbyter from the parish of Baucalis in Alexandria. Basically a theological debate, eventually the dispute involved personal feuds between bishops and theologians, conflicts between traditionalism and unrestrained speculation, and the politics of Roman emperors who needed a united church to preserve a united empire. The outset of the controversy, probably in about the year 319, was caused by Arius's preaching. According to Arius's message, only God the Father is eternal and unoriginated. The Logos, the preexistent Christ, is a creature, created out of nothing, and had a beginning. Arius believed that there was when he was not—thus the Arian slogan. This means that the Logos is not eternal, he is strange to the divine nature. Indeed, Arius taught that the Logos neither sees nor knows the Father completely. The power of God then at work in Jesus is not the eternal divine power itself but a limited and lower hierarchy. The titles "God" and "Son of God" are courtesy titles. The Logos is capable of change, but God, foreknowing that he would remain good, gave him in anticipation the glory which as man, and in consequence of his virtue, he would afterward possess. For Arius, Jesus is a demigod, neither fully God nor fully man. He becomes God only in the way that every saint may be deified. Arius's teaching has antecedents in Origen's thought, but he eliminated Origen's view of eternal generation and pushed his subordination to extreme lengths. As a result, Arius blurred Christianity and paganism.

Although most Arian literature has perished, a letter of Arius to Eusebius, bishop of Nicomedia, written around 319 (see Chapter 2), and a letter or a confession of faith to Alexander of Alexandria, his bishop, dating from the year 320 (see Chapter 3), give his views early in the controversy and show how he and his adherents claimed that they were teaching nothing new but following Lucian of Antioch, who died in the year 312, and the traditions of the bishop of Alexandria himself.

Alexander of Alexandria

Alexander's response to Arius can be outlined from letters written after Arius's views became known. Alexander's letter to Alexander of Thessalonica, or possibly Alexander of Byzantium, from the year 324, is an excellent source for Alexander of Alexandria's thought (see Chapter 4). Alexander was an Origenist. He held to the divinity of the Logos, eternally generated by the Father. Still he regarded the Logos as a distinct *hypostasis.* Alexander apparently thought of God as two *hypostases*, sharing the same nature. The Father alone is unoriginate, but the Son is co-eternal with the Father, since God cannot be without the Word. The Sonship of the Logos is real and natural.

Alexander of Alexandria probably wished to stay out of a theological debate, but this option was not granted to him. Thus he summoned a council, which condemned Arius and sent him into exile. As the controversy deepened between the years 321 and 324, Arius found supporters outside Egypt. Eusebius, bishop of Nicomedia, an old friend and fellow pupil of Lucian, befriended him. Arius also secured the assistance of the influential historian Eusebius, who was bishop of Caesarea.

The Council of Antioch

By this time Constantine became the sole emperor of the Roman Empire by defeating Licinius. Constantine had been moving ever closer to Christianity, in part because he saw it as a means to unify the empire. Now he found that Christianity was in danger of splitting because of a theological question he could not understand. The emperor urged Alexander and Arius to stop their philosophical bickering and live in peace. Not surprisingly, such a plea did not settle the problem. Hosius, the theological adviser to Constantine, presided over a council held in Antioch in the early months of 325. This council was strongly anti-Arian. It censured Eusebius of Caesarea as a follower of Arius, drew up a confessional formula which was in agreement with the position of Alexander of Alexandria, and sent out a letter announcing the resolutions of the council, and setting forth the council's faith in a creedal form. A Syriac text of this letter was discovered about 75 years ago, so it is possible to gain a trustworthy picture of what occurred in Antioch in 325 (see Chapter 5). Thus it is now known that Eusebius of Caesarea was under a condemnation from the early months of 325.

The Council of Nicaea

As a result of events in the east, Emperor Constantine decided to call a universal council of the church to settle the dispute. The synodal letter from Antioch makes mention of the synod to be held in Ancyra. But the site was transferred to Nicaea before the beginning of the council. The council was opened by Constantine in June of 325 with about three hundred bishops present, most of whom were from the east. Unfortunately, no full report of this first ecumenical council is extant. Still, it is possible to follow the main events. Probably the bishops were soon divided into three groups: Arius and his supporters; his opponents, including Athanasius the future bishop of Alexandria who came as Alexander's attendant; and a majority of Eastern bishops who wished to maintain the traditional Logos theology of the church without taking a strongly anti-Arian position. It seems that quite soon the council determined Arius's theology was unacceptable.

The creed of the council (see Chapter 6) declared that the Son is begotten and not made. The Son is true God, not "God" by way of a courtesy title. Those who believe that the Father preexisted before the Son or that the Son came into existence from nothing or is subject to change were anathematized. The Council of Nicaea clearly went on record against Arius and with the views of Alexander about the divinity and immutability of the Logos. It is not clear what the council intended to teach by the phrase "from the substance [ousia] of the Father" and homoousios with the Father. Both were unscriptural and employed with some reluctance. The latter phrase was placed in the creed by the emperor Constantine, probably with Hosius's guidance. Literally it means "of the same ousia" (substance). But did the council mean this in a generic sense? This is how Origen had used it, as has been indicated above, and there were parallels in other Christian authors. Or did Nicaea intend the term to describe a numerical identity of substance? The former interpretation is probably true. The word was selected at Nicaea to express that the Son was fully God. This agrees with what all the historical sources convey: The issue at Nicaea was the Son's co-eternity with the Father, not the unity of the Godhead. This would become clear in the work of Athanasius (see below). One of the assets of the word homoousios—and this led to its acceptance— was that different groups were able to interpret it in ways compatible with their own theology. As far as Constantine was concerned, this was agreeable. Constantine was amenable to tolerating a variety of groups, as long as they accepted his creed and each other. In addition to the creed, the council turned to a number of problems that were divisive in the church: a settlement of a schism in the Egyptian church, the date of Easter, the status of sees, and church discipline. These canons, while not dealing with the doctrine of God, are included in this volume to show the complete work of the council (see Chapter 7).

Eusebius of Caesarea

Eusebius, with the emperor's support, cleared himself at Nicaea of the censure placed upon him at Antioch some months earlier. Eusebius was more of a historian than a theologian. His theological views reflected the subordinationist strand in Origen. For Eusebius of Caesarea, the Father was an indivisible monad beyond reality, the cause of all things, self-existent and without beginning (The Demonstration of the Gospel 4.1.145). The Logos, a distinct hypostasis, begotten before all ages, is the Father's intermediary for creating. The Logos has no direct contact with the Father's being. Although the Logos differs from all creatures and has the image of God, he is entitled to be called God (Dem. Gos. 4.2.1). But the Logos is not eternal with the Father.

The unity of the Son with the Father consists of sharing his identical glory (*Ecclesiastical Theology* 3.19). Eusebius was not an Arian, but his indiscreet statements and general approach disclosed a great distance between him and Alexander of Alexandria, and later between him and Athanasius. Therefore, to prove his orthodoxy, Eusebius at Nicaea brought forth the baptismal creed of his own church. This creed was accepted as orthodox. There is available a letter which Eusebius of Caesarea sent to his diocese soon after the council, to explain his role at Nicaea and how he was able to sign the final text of the creed (see Chapter 8 of this volume). Eusebius shares with his diocese how he, on the basis of the emperor's interpretation, could accept *homoousios* and finally the creed itself after long scrutiny. It is unlikely that all at Nicaea accepted the term in the way Eusebius did. Eusebius's implication that the creed of Nicaea was the baptismal creed of Caesarea with additions is now rejected by scholars.

Constantine and Constantius

At the council the emperor himself had spoken, and no one in the emperor's lifetime moved against his creed. In a real sense the council was a product of the emperor. The Council of Nicaea was invited by the emperor. Meetings and doctrinal discussions were in his hands. A new chapter in church and state relations had opened. The differing interpretations of what the council was teaching may have been an advantage initially, for with imperial pressure all but two bishops finally subscribed to the creed. But with the passing of time and the removal of Constantine from the scene, Nicaea's lack of clarity became a weakness.

After the council, Constantine's policy of unification appeared to be successful. Even Arians found ways to win back favor (see Chapter 9). Constantine's creed was sacrosanct, but a coalition opposed to the teaching of Nicaea moved to dispose a number of the council's supporters, including Athanasius, Alexander of Alexandria's successor who became bishop of Alexandria in 328. A number of councils were held that tried to move away from the Nicene Creed by producing moderate formulas, critical of Arianism but omitting the phrase *homoousios*. When Constantine's son Constantius, who leaned toward Arianism, ruled as sole emperor between the years 350 and 361, obvious efforts were made to undo the decisions of Nicaea. It was not until the year 381, at the Council of Constantinople, that the Nicene faith finally triumphed. The tumultuous period between Nicaea and Constantinople saw the theological work of Athanasius of Alexandria and the three Cappadocian fathers, Basil of Caesarea, Gregory of Nazianzus, and Gregory of Nyssa, who were responsible for the victory of the Nicene faith.

Athanasius

Athanasius, bishop of Alexandria from 328 until his death in 373, was the great defender of the decision at Nicaea. His commitment to the faith of Nicaea was unalterable. He was able to use a variety of means to advance his cause, including theological pressure. Consistent, even cautious, he was able to distinguish the major issue from secondary concerns. Thus he could be compromising in terminology when required. One of his major accomplishments was a Council in Alexandria in 362, which recognized that what was critical was not the language but the meaning it expressed. Because of the work of this council, the confusion over the possible meaning of *hypostasis* and *ousia* was cleared up. The formula of one *hypostasis* was endorsed as a means of stating the unity of nature between Father and Son. This work enabled a great number of the moderates to come together with Athanasius and his followers and secured the final success of what Nicaea sought to preserve. Athanasius saved Nicaea. In the process, he was expelled from Alexandria five times over several decades. He was persecuted, but finally he prevailed over heretics and emperors.

For Athanasius, the major issue in the quarrel with Arius was the nature of salvation. Salvation he believed was possible only on one condition, namely, the Son of God was made man in Jesus so that we might become God. This means the Logos must be eternal, really God, who appeared in Jesus. God is Father only because he is the Father of the Son. Therefore the Son is without beginning. Eternally the Father has the Son. The Son is the eternal Son of the Father. The Father is the eternal Father of the Son. Only if they are co-eternal can Jesus, in whom the Logos is present, give us eternal life. This likeness and unity are in respect to the Son's substance. Athanasius spoke of the oneness of being between Father and Son. Jesus can make us like God, which means, for Athanasius, make us immortal and give us eternal knowledge. Not the highest of all created beings can give us real salvation. Thus God himself must save human beings. Only Christ as true man suffering the curse of sin and as true God can overcome death. No half-God, no hero, no relative power could accomplish man's salvation. Consequently, Athanasius taught that the Holy Spirit must be as divine as Christ if he is to unite individuals with Christ. Here Athanasius moved beyond Nicaea, drawing out the implications of the Nicene statement in stating the equal status of Father, Son, and Holy Spirit. Athanasius's teaching and his estimate of Arius can be observed in the first book of his *Orations against the Arians*. This work also gives the text of Arius's *Thalia* (see Chapter 10). There has been some difference of scholarly opinion about the date of the composition of Athanasius's *against the Arians*. Probably a date around the years 356 to 358 is accurate for the first three books. The prevailing opinion is that book 4 is not by Athanasius.

Gregory of Nazianzus and Gregory of Nyssa

Among the groupings of Eastern bishops formed after the Council of Nicaea was a large party of moderates. Unhappy with the term *homoousios*, they preferred such phrases as "like the Father in all things," or they spoke of the deity of the Word and the likeness of substance between the Word and Father. As time passed, this group moved closer to the teaching of Athanasius. A decisive event in this movement was the Council of Alexandria in 362. This coalition became known as the Homoiousians, from the Greek word *homoiousios* (literally "of like substance"), or more unfortunately as semi-Arians—a misleading term. Gregory of Nazianzus and Gregory of Nyssa, two of the Cappadocian fathers, whose writings are represented in this volume, came out of this homoiousian tradition. They made possible the agreements which led to the Council of Constantinople in 381. The theology—some would prefer philosophy—of the Cappadocians is complex and abstract, but it provided a formula which reunited the church. Their debt to Aristotelian and Neoplatonic thought is undeniable. They teach that the Godhead exists simultaneously in three modes of being or *hypostases*. All three have one nature, God. Subordination is carefully eliminated, but they teach that the Father is the source or principle of the Godhead. In a sense the Father causes the other two beings. To describe how the one substance can be present at the same time in three, the analogy of a universal and its particulars is used. The difference between *ousia* and *hypostasis* is the difference between universal and particular. Each *hypostasis* of the Godhead is set by its appropriate characteristics, just as each man represents the universal man. It should be noted that the weakness of this analogy was recognized by the Cappadocians.

Gregory of Nazianzus especially made sharp distinctions between these concepts. The idea *of hypostasis* was more completely analyzed than it had been by Athanasius. The stress is on the three *hypostases* which share the one same nature. Both Gregorys speak of the divine action that begins with the Father, proceeds through the Son, and is completed in the Spirit. One identical energy passes through all three. Nevertheless, the number three is real for both these fathers. Each of the three has its special characteristic. So much emphasis was placed on the threeness that critics claimed that the Cappadocians used the term *homoousios* in only a generic sense. Such a charge does not take seriously the entire work of the Cappadocians whose contribution was great. Their view of the Trinity represented a high point with its clear teaching of the *homoousion* of the Spirit. They showed the entire Eastern church how it was possible to interpret *homoousios* in the light of *hotnoiousios*, and made reunion a reality in the year 381 with the Council of Constantinople. This council removed the condemnations added to the Nicene Creed, since they did not apply to the new terminology of the Cappadocians, and said more about the Holy Spirit in light of the writings of Athanasius, Gregory of Nazianzus, and Gregory of Nyssa. At Constantinople a coherent doctrine of God with the formulation of three *hypostases* and one *ousia* was achieved. Refinements and nuances of thought were yet to occur, but the trinitarian controversy had ended. Arius and his followers were excluded. What the Christian community had rejected was clear.

In this collection two writings of the Cappadocian theologians are included. Gregory, bishop of Nazianzus, for a short time was bishop of Constantinople. He was a leading figure at the Council of Constantinople in 381. During the previous year he delivered at Constantinople five theological orations to protect his congregation against Arianism. These sermons represent a refined discussion of the trinitarian doctrine. The third oration shows the unity of nature in the three divine persons and especially the divinity of the Logos. (This sermon is Chapter 11).

Gregory, bishop of Nyssa, the younger brother of Basil of Caesarea was a speculative theologian of the highest order. He took part in the second ecumenical council at Constantinople. Among his dogmatic works is a tract entitled "That There Are Not Three Gods," addressed to a certain Ablabius, on the question of why it is not proper to speak of three Gods when the divinity of the Father, Son, and Holy Spirit is recognized. (This treatise, probably written about the year 390, is Chapter 12.)

THE FIFTH CENTURY—AUGUSTINE

Even a casual glance at the authors examined here discloses a preoccupation with Eastern theologians and churchmen. This is not surprising, for the trinitarian controversy was a doctrinal contention within the Eastern church, although its implications were patent for the entire Christian community. No collection of significant patristic writings dealing with the Trinity would be complete without the work of the greatest theologian of the Western patristic church, Augustine, bishop of Hippo in North Africa, who molded Western theology from his day to the present. Augustine was influenced by Neoplatonism. He built on the earlier suggestions of Ambrose, bishop of Milan from 374 to 397, and C. Marius Victorinus, the Christian Neoplatonist who lived in Rome in the latter fourth century. In his treatise, *On the Trinity*, composed between 399 and 419, Augustine employing these resources brought Western trinitarian thought to new heights of theological reflection. Without exaggeration Augustine must be considered one of the greatest intellectuals, not only of the Western church but of Western civilization as well. He ranks with an elite group of very few other theologians.

Like other Western theologians, Augustine was more interested in the unity of God than in the three *hypostases*. He repeatedly stated there is one God, the Trinity—Father, Son, and Holy Spirit, who are at once distinct, numerically one in substance. Augustine accepts this as a given of revelation. His starting point is the divine substance. He emphasizes the unity of the Trinity; all subordinationism is ruled out. Each of the three persons from the vantage point of substance is identical with the others or with the divine substance itself. There is one action and will of the Trinity. All persons are inseparable and so operate. The weak point in Augustine's trinitarian theology was the apparent obliteration of the several roles of the three persons. He was aware of the problem. His answer was that each of the persons possesses the divine nature in a particular way. Thus it is proper to attribute to each the role appropriate by virtue of his origin. Augustine sees the distinction in the mutual relations within the Godhead. Identical in divine substance, the Father is distinguished as Father because he begets the Son. The Son is distinguished as Son because he is begotten. The Spirit is distinguished from the Father because he is their common gift, a kind of communion of the Father and the Son. Augustine never found an adequate explanation of the procession of the Spirit. He was not able to illustrate how this procession differs from the generation of the Son. He was convinced that the Spirit is the mutual love of the Father and the Son, the bond which unites them. For Augustine, the Spirit is the Spirit of both Father and Son. He clearly taught that the Spirit proceeds from both the Father and the Son (*filioque*), the doctrine of double procession, which later would cause such heated theological struggles between the Eastern church and the Western church. One of Augustine's most original suggestions in trinitarian theology was the use of analogy, especially his analogy based on the structure of the human soul. In the work *On the Trinity*, Augustine makes clear his view that these analogies have limits. They do not prove the Trinity; the mystery is not removed. Yet they are useful. For example, Augustine speaks of the Father, Son, and Holy Spirit as analogous to he who loves, that which is loved, and the power of love. He also refers to the Trinity as analogous to memory, intelligence, and will. Thus he uses the Trinity to give analogically a description of God as a person. Since God is a person, that is, a unity, all his acts toward the outside are always acts of the whole Trinity. Since the substance of all things is love—in its threefold appearance of he who loves, that which is loved, and the power of love—everything created by God has traces of the Trinity. Book 9, one of the most original parts of *On the Trinity*, is a discussion of the human mind as a created image of the Trinity. (It is included in this volume as Chapter 13.)

SUMMARY

With the Cappadocians in the east and Augustine in the west, patristic thought on the doctrine of God obtains its finished form. In one sense there has been much movement from the unrefined witness of the Apostolic Fathers to the polished, philosophically sophisticated writings of these later fathers. From another perspective the movement is not all that extreme. The threefold pattern evidenced within the New Testament itself has been preserved. Judgments on the development and final formation of the doctrine of the Trinity vary. For some it is a high point of theological and intellectual achievement that preserved the uniqueness of Christianity and allowed it to enter, and finally win, the Greco-Roman world. Others have seen the developments traced in this volume as a capitulation of the biblical revelation to a foreign system from which Christianity has still not yet escaped. Whatever position is taken in this regard, it is obvious that historical Christianity cannot be understood without a knowledge of how its doctrine of God acquired its final form in the patristic church. It is the intention of this volume to allow those writers of the early church to speak and tell their own story.

In the translations that follow, the Greek word *hypostasis* has been transliterated into English. *Ousia*, or *substantia* in Latin, has been rendered "substance." Whenever possible, biblical quotations have been identified and translated from the patristic text. Thus they should not be expected to agree with any particular translation of the Bible.

2

Arius's Letter to Eusebius of Nicomedia

(1) To a most longed-for lord, a faithful man of God, orthodox Eusebius; Arius, who is unjustly persecuted by Pope Alexander on account of the all-prevailing truth which you also protect, sends greetings in the Lord.

(2) Since my father Ammonius was coming into Nicomedia, it appeared to me reasonable and fitting to address you through him and in like manner to remind your innate love and disposition, which you have toward the brothers because of God and his Christ, that the bishop greatly pillages us and persecutes us, and invoking all things moves against us, so that he might drive us as godless men from the city. All this is because we do not agree with him when he states in public, "Always God always Son," " At the same time Father, at the same time Son," "The Son ingenerably coexists with God," "Ever-begotten, ungenerated-created, neither in thought nor in some moment of time does God proceed the Son," "Always God always Son," "The Son is from God himself."

(3) And since Eusebius, your brother in Caesarea, and Theodotus, Paulinus, Athanasius, Gregory, Aetius, and all the bishops throughout the East, say that God without beginning exists before the Son, an anathema was pronounced against them—except Philogonius, Hellanicus, and Macareius—heretical and ignorant men, who speak about the Son. Some of them say that he is a belching, others an emanation, and still others alike-ingenerate.

(4) If the heretics should threaten us with myriads of deaths, we are not able even to hear these impieties.

But what do we say and think? What have we taught and what do we teach? That the Son is not unbegotten or a portion of the unbegotten in any manner or from any substratum, but that by the will and counsel of the Father he subsisted before times and ages, full of grace and truth, God, only-begotten, unchangeable. (5) And before he was begotten or created or defined or established, he was not. For he was not unbegotten. But we are persecuted because we say, "The Son has a beginning, but God is without beginning." Because of this we are persecuted because we say, "The Son has a beginning, but God is without beginning." We are persecuted because we say, "He is from nothing." But we speak thus inasmuch as he is neither part of God nor from any substratum. On account of this we are persecuted. You know the rest. I pray that you are strong in the Lord, recalling our afflictions, fellow pupil of Lucian, truly "Eusebius."

3

Arius's Letter to Alexander of Alexandria

(1) The presbyters and deacons send greetings in the Lord to our blessed pope and bishop, Alexander.

(2) Our faith, from our ancestors, which we have learned also from you, is this. We know one God—alone unbegotten, alone everlasting, alone without beginning, alone true, alone possessing immortality, alone wise, alone good, alone master, judge of all, manager, director, immutable and unchangeable, just and good, God of Law, Prophets, and New Testament—who begot an only-begotten Son before eternal times, through whom he made the ages and everything. But he begot him not in appearance but in truth, having submitted him to his own will, an immutable and unchangeable perfect creature of God, (3) but not as one of the creatures—an offspring, but not as one of those born—nor as Valentinus decreed that the offspring of the Father is an emanation, nor as Manes propounded that the offspring of the Father is part of the same substance, nor as Sabellius, who divides the monad, says "Father-and-Son," nor as Hieracas believes a light from a light as a lamp divided into two; nor is he the one who was before, later begotten or created into a Son as you yourself also, Blessed Pope, very often have forbidden throughout the midst of the church and in council those who teach these things. But, as we say, he was created by the will of God before times and ages, and he received life, being, and glories from the Father as the Father has shared them with him. (4) For the Father, having given to him the inheritance of all, did not deprive himself of those things which he has in himself without generation, for he is the source of all. Thus there are three *hypostases*. God being the cause of all is without beginning, most alone; but the Son, begotten by the Father, created and founded before the ages, was not before he was begotten. Rather, the Son begotten timelessly before everything, alone was caused to subsist by the Father. For he is not everlasting or co-everlasting or unbegotten with the Father. Nor does he have being with the Father, as certain individuals mention things relatively and bring into the discussion two unbegotten causes. But God is thus before all as a monad and cause. Therefore he is also before the Son, as

we have learned from you when you preached throughout the midst of the church.

(5) Therefore, insofar as he has from God being, glories, and life, and all things have been handed over to him, thus God is his cause. For he, as his God and being before him, rules him. But if "from him" [Rom. 11:36] and "from the womb" [Ps. 110:3] and "I came from the Father and I come" [John 16:28] are thought by some to signify that he is a part of him and an emanation, the Father will be according to them compounded, divided, mutable and a body, and, as far as they are concerned, the incorporeal God suffers things suitable to the body.

I pray that you are well in the Lord, Blessed Pope.

Arius, Aeithales, Achillas, Carpones, Sarmates, and Arius—presbyters.

Euzoius, Lucius, Julius, Menas, Helladius, Gaius—deacons.

Bishops Secundus of Pentapolis, Theonas of Libya, and Pistus.

4

Alexander of Alexandria's Letter to Alexander of Thessalonica

To Alexander, a most honored brother united in the soul, Alexander sends greetings in the Lord.

(1) The ambitious and covetous calculation of rascally men has produced plots against the apparently greater dioceses. Through intricate pretenses such individuals are attacking the orthodox faith of the church. Driven wild by the devil at work in them for pleasures at hand, they skipped away from every piety and trampled on the fear of God's judgment. (2) It was necessary for me who am suffering to make clear to Your Reverence these matters so that you might be on guard against such persons, lest some of them dare to come even into your dioceses, either through themselves (for cheats are equal to dissemble for deceit) or through basely refined rescripts, which are able to snatch away a person intent on a simple and pure faith.

(3) At any rate, Arius and Achillas have just now entered into a conspiracy, and they have revealed the covetousness of Colluthus, to a much worse degree than even he himself. For Colluthus in bringing charges against them found an excuse for his own ambitious course of action. But they, when they saw him making Christ a source of gain, were not patient to remain as subjects of the church; after constructing for themselves robbers' caves, they held in them incessant assemblies, slandering Christ and us by night and day. (4) They denounced every pious apostolic doctrine; they organized in a Jewish manner a work group contending against Christ. They deny the divinity of our Savior, and proclaim him equal to all. Singling out every expression of his economy for salvation and of his humiliation for our sake, they attempt from them to bring together the proclamation of their own impiety, and from the beginning they turn away from expressions of his divinity and from words of his indescribable glory with the Father. (5) Confirming the impious doctrine of the Greeks and Jews about Christ, as much as possible they pursue praise for themselves. They undertake all those things for which others laugh at us, arousing daily strife and persecutions. They organize this court action through an accusation of disorderly women, whom they have led into error.

They are tearing Christianity into pieces by the indecent running around of their young women on every street. The seamless robe of Christ which the executioners resolved not to divide, they dared to split. (6) Therefore, after we understood what was befitting their life and unholy attempt—and we did this slowly because it was concealed—we expelled them altogether from the church that worships Christ's divinity.

(7) And by running to fellow ministers of one mind with us, they attempted to turn them against us. They dissembled a reputation under the show of peace and unity, but in truth they were eager to carry certain of the ministers away into their disease by fair words, and they requested from them rescripts that were too wordy, so that by reading them, in addition to those deceived by them, they would make them both unrepentant in those things in which they were mistaken and destroyed in impiety. This they did on the grounds that they have bishops who agree and are of one mind with them. (8) They do not confess to them those things which they wickedly taught and effected, on account of which they were expelled by us, but they either hand them on in silence or deceive, obscuring them with fabricated words and writings.

(9) Concealing their ruinous teaching with sermons that are too persuasive and of low quality, they seize the person involved in deceit. They do not even desist from slandering our orthodox faith in the presence of everyone. So it happens that certain persons subscribing to their writings admit them into the church. I think that the great slander belongs to our fellow ministers who allow this—for the apostolic rule does not assent to this—who thereby inflame slanderous action against Christ by those who oppose us.

(10) For this reason, with no delay, I aroused myself, beloved, to make clear to you the unbelief of those who say, "There was once when the Son of God was not" and "He who before was not, later came into existence; and when he came into existence, he became as every human being is by nature." They say, "For God made all things from nothing," including even the Son of God with the creation of all rational and irrational creatures. In accord with this, they even say that he is of a mutable nature, capable of both virtue and evil, and with their supposition "from nothing" they destroy the divine Scriptures' witness that he always is, which Scriptures indicate the immutability of the Word and the divinity of the Wisdom of the Word, which is Christ. The wretches state, "Then we too are able to become sons of God, just as he." For it was written, "I have begotten and raised up sons" [Isa. 1:2]. (12) And when they add the statement from the text "But they rejected me," which does not belong to the nature of the Savior, who is of an immutable nature, they abandon every reverence. They say that God, knowing about him by foreknowledge and prevision, would not reject him and chose him from all. (13) For he does not have by nature something special from other sons (for they say that no one is by nature Son of God), nor does he have some distinctive property in relation to God, but he, being of a mutable nature, because of the diligence

of his manners and not rejecting his training for the inferior status—he was chosen. (14) As if both a Paul and a Peter would persist at improvement, then their sonship would differ in no way from his. To explain this crazy teaching, they act insultingly toward Scripture and propose the passage in the Psalms about Christ which reads, "You have loved righteousness and hated injustice; on account of this, God, your God, anointed you with the oil of great joy beyond your partners" [Ps. 45:7].

(15) Therefore, concerning the fact that the Son of God came into existence from nothing and that not was there once when he was not, John the evangelist instructed sufficiently, writing about him, "the only-begotten Son who is in the bosom of the Father" [John 1:18]. For the divine teacher in foresight shows that the two things, the Father and the Son, are inseparable from one another. There he specified that he is in the bosom of the Father. (16) And in regard to the fact that the Word of God is not numbered with those who come into existence from nothing, the same John declares that all things came into existence through him [John 1:3]. For John makes clear the Word's distinctive *hypostasis*, saying, "In the beginning was the Word and the Word was with God and the Word was God. All things came into existence through him, and without him nothing came into existence" [John 1:1, 3]. (17) If all things came into existence through him, how is it that he who gave being to the ones who came into existence once was not? For the Word, that which makes, is not defined so as to be of the same nature as those who came into existence, if he was in the beginning and all things came into existence through him and he made them from nothing. (18) For that which is and is exceedingly aloof seems opposite to those who came into existence from nothing. (19) This shows that no distance exists between the Father and Son, and that the soul is not able, as far as any thought is concerned, to form an image of this relationship of Father and Son. But the fact that the universe was fashioned from nothing has a newer *hypostasis* and a fresh origin, since all things received such origination by the Father through the Son. Since the most orthodox John saw that "was" is far from the Word of God and raised high beyond the thought of originated things, he would not speak of the Word's origin and creation, and he did not dare to specify in equivalent syllables the maker with those who came into existence—and not because the Son is unbegotten, for the Father is the one unbegotten, but because the indescribable *hypostasis* of the only-begotten God is beyond the sharpened apprehension of the evangelists, and perhaps of the angels. I do not think that those persons who dare to inquire about this, as far as these matters, give thought for the orthodox faith, because they are not willing to hear "Seek not that which is too difficult for you, and do not inquire about that which is too high for you" [Ecclus. 3:21]. (20) For if the knowledge of many things incomparably more imperfect than this is hidden with regard to human apprehension—such thoughts are in Paul "which things God has prepared for those who love him, eye knew not and ear heard not, and have not

entered into the heart of man" [1 Cor. 2:9], and God said to Abraham that the stars are not able to be counted [Gen. 15:5], and still he says, "The sands of the sea and drops of rains, who will count them?" [Ecclus. 1:2]—how does anyone meddle with the *hypostasis* of the Word of God unless he happens to be seized with a melancholic disposition? (21) Concerning this, the prophetic Spirit says, "Who will describe his generation?" [Isa. 53:8]. Thus even our Savior himself, in showing kindness to those who were the pillars of the whole world, was eager to rid them of the knowledge of this knowledge. Therefore he said to all of them that it was beyond nature for them to apprehend this, and that the knowledge of this most divine mystery is the Father's alone. He said, "No one knows who the Son is except the Father, and no one knows the Father except the Son" [Matt. 11:27]. I think that concerning this the Father said, "My mystery is for me" [Isa. 24:16]. (22) But the phrase "from nothing" shows at once that it is crazy to think that the Son came into existence from nothing with the temporal purpose. This is true even if silly individuals are ignorant of the madness of their own voice. The expression "he was not" is necessarily in reference either to time or to some interval of the age. (23) Therefore it is true that all things came into existence through him; it is clear that every age, time, interval, and "when," in which the expression "he was not" is found, came into existence through him. How is it not incredible to say that once he was not, he who made times, ages, and seasons, with which "he was not" is united? It is incomprehensible and totally ignorant to state that the cause of anything having come into existence is itself later than its generation.

(24) For according to them, that interval preceded the Wisdom of God which fashioned all things—an interval in which they say that the Son was not begotten by the Father. Thus, according to them, Scripture played false in proclaiming that he is the firstborn of every creature [Col. 1:15]. (25) Then in harmony with this teaching Paul shouts in his loudest voice, saying about him, "Whom he placed as heir of all through whom he also made the ages" [Heb. 1:2] but also, ' 'In him all things were created, those in heaven and those on earth, and seen and unseen, whether principalities or powers or dominions or thrones, all things were created through him and for him, and he himself is before all things" [Col. 1:16-17]. (26) Therefore, since the argument "from nothing" seems most impious, it is necessary that the Father is always the Father. But he is Father of the always present Son, on account of whom he is called Father; and with the Son always present with him, the Father is always perfect, unfailing in goodness, who begot the only-begotten Son not temporally or in an interval or from nothing. (27) Why is it not unjust to say that once the Wisdom of God was not—the Wisdom who says, "I was with him as one united to him, I was the one in whom he rejoiced" [Prov. 8:30]— or that once the power of God was not, or once his Word was mutilated, or any other things from which the Son is known and the Father is designated? To say that the brightness of the glory is not, destroys completely

the archetypal light of which it is the brightness. And if the image of God was not always, it is clear that he whose image it is, is not always. (28) But also with the nonexistence of the express image of the /hypostasis of God, he who is imaged by him is destroyed. Thus it is possible to see that the Sonship of the Savior has nothing in common with the sonship of the others. (29) Just as his inexpressible *hypostasis* has been shown in incomparable excess to excel all with whom he himself has been granted being, so that his sonship, possessing by nature his paternal divinity, differs by an unmentionable excess from those who have been adopted as sons through him by adoption. He possesses an immutable nature, being perfect and in want of nothing, but they who are subject to change in either of two ways need assistance from him. (30) Why might the Wisdom of God be able to advance, or what might absolute truth be able to add? Or how might God the Word be able to be improved, or life or the true light? But if this is so, by how much does a great occurrence beyond nature happen, namely, that wisdom at some time becomes capable of folly, or that the power of God is connected with weakness, or that reason is dimmed by the absence of reason, or that darkness is mingled with true light? The apostle states of his own accord, "What is there in common between light and darkness, or what is there between Christ and Belial?" [2 Cor. 6:14-15]. Solomon declares that as far as any thought, *it* would be impossible that the ways of a snake be found on a rock [Prov. 30:19], which according to Paul is Christ [1 Cor. 10:4]. But they, men and angels, being his creatures, also received blessings to advance in virtues, disciplined by his customary commands so as not to sin. (31) Therefore our Lord, being Son of the Father by nature, is worshiped. And those who have put off the spirit of slavery, from acts of virtue and progress, and who received the spirit of adoption as sons, become sons by adoption being shown a kindness by the Son, who is Son by nature.

(32) Therefore Paul made known his legitimate, distinctive, essential, and special sonship, saying about God, ". . . Who did not spare his own son but delivered him for us" (who are clearly not sons by nature) [Rom. 8:32]. (33) For to make a distinction between those who are not his own, Paul said that he was his own Son. And in the Gospel, "This is my beloved son in whom I am well pleased" [Matt. 3:17]. In the Psalms the Savior says, "The Lord said to me, 'You are my son'" [Ps. 2:7]. Explaining the true Sonship, he indicates that there are not some other legitimate sons besides himself. (34) What does the phrase "from the womb before morning I begot you" [Ps. 110:10, LXX] indicate? Is it not plainly the essential sonship of the paternal birth, which obtains this not by attention to manners and practice of progress but by the characteristic property of nature? But that the adoption of the rational ones as sons is not according to nature but by aptitude of manners and God's gift, and liable to change, the Word knows, "for the sons of God having seen the daughters of men took them to themselves as wives" etc. [Gen. 6:2], and we were taught

that God spoke through Isaiah, "I have begotten sons and exalted them, but they rejected me" [Isa. 1:2].

(35) Although I am able to say many things, beloved, I pass them by, thinking that it is burdensome to remind teachers of one mind of more items. For you yourselves, taught by God, are not ignorant that the teaching, which has just now risen up against the church's piety, is of Ebion and Artemas and is an emulation of Paul of Samosata's teaching at Antioch. He was excommunicated from the church by a synod and judgment of all the bishops. (36) Lucian, who succeeded him, remained excommunicated from three bishops during many years. Now among us have grown up those "from nothing" who drained the dregs of the impiety of Ebion, Artemas, and Paul: their hidden offsets, I mean Arius, Achillas, and the assembly of rogues with them. (37) The three bishops in Syria—I do not know how they were appointed— through agreement with them inflamed matters even more. Concerning their judgment, let it be referred to your examination. They keep in their memory statements about the Savior's sufferings, humblings, emptying, and so-called poverty, which by addition the Savior accepted on our account. They quote these as evidence for impugning his highest and essential divinity; they forget the words indicating his essential glory, nobility, and dwelling with the Father. "I and the Father are one" [John 10:30]. (38) The Lord says this, not proclaiming himself the Father or explaining that the two natures in the *hypostasis* are one, but saying that the Son of the Father is disposed by nature accurately to save the paternal likeness. Thus he took from his nature an impression of his likeness in all regards and is an unchangeable image of the Father and can express the image of the archetype. (39) The Lord made this plain to Philip, who was desiring then to see—the Lord to whom Philip said, "Show us the Father"—by saying, "The one who has seen me has seen the Father" [John 14:9], just as if the Father is seen through a spotless and living mirror of his divine image. (40) The most holy ones say the same thing in the Psalms: "In your light we shall see light" [Ps. 36:9]. Therefore, "He who honors the Son, honors the Father" [John 5:23], and fairly. For every impious statement dared to be said against the Son has a reference against the Father.

(41) And what, in the things I am about to write, hereafter is wondrous, beloved, if I shall declare the false accusations against me and our most pious people? For drawn up against the divinity of the Son of God, they do not refrain from speaking unpleasant insults against us. Nor do they think certain of the ancients are worthy to be compared with themselves, nor do they suffer to be equal to teachers with whom we have been associated from childhood. But they suppose that not even one of all the present fellow ministers has a part of wisdom. They say that they only are wise, prudent, and discoverers of doctrines, and that to them alone have been disclosed those very things which are disposed by nature to come into consideration of no one else under the sun.

(42) O unholy, blind, and excessive madness, melancholic, exalted, empty boasting and Satanic arrogance that has leaped into their unholy souls. (43) The devout lucidity of the ancient Scriptures has not stopped them, nor has the piety about Christ agreed to by their fellow ministers impaired their audaciousness against him. Not even the evil spirits suffer their profaneness, for they shun saying a slanderous word against the Son of God. (44) Therefore, according to the ability present in us, let these things be supplied to those who have thrown dust on Christ with boorish barking and have attempted to slander our piety for him. The discoverers of silly stories say that we, turning away from the impious and unscriptural slander against Christ that he is "from nothing," teach two unbegotten beings. These uneducated persons say that it is necessary that there be one of these two alternatives: either to think that he is "from nothing" or to say that certainly there are two unbegotten beings. These unpracticed persons do not know that great is the distance between an unbegotten Father and those created by him from nothing as both rational and irrational. (45) The only-begotten nature is in the middle of these, the nature by which the Father of the Word of God made all things from nothing, the Word being of the Father, of whom it was written as the Lord himself bore witness saying, "He who loves the Father loves also the Son begotten from him" [1 John 5:1].

(46) Thus concerning this, we believe—as it seems best to the apostolic church—in one unbegotten Father, who of his being has no cause, who is immutable and unchangeable, always according to the same things in the same state, neither receiving progress nor diminution, who is giver of the Law, Prophets, and Gospels, who is Lord of patriarchs, apostles, and all the saints; and in one Lord Jesus Christ, the only-begotten Son of God, begotten not from nothing but from the Father who is, not according to the likenesses of bodies by dissections or emanations from divisions, as it appears to Sabellius and Valentinus, but inexplicably and indescribably, according to him who said, as we set forth above, "Who will describe his generation?" [Isa. 53:8], since his *hypostasis* happens to be beyond investigation by every originated nature, just as the Father himself is beyond investigation because *the* nature of rational ones does not allow the knowledge of the divine generation by the Father. (47) Men moved by the Spirit of truth need not learn these things from me, since the voice of Christ echoes in us and anticipates us, teaching, "No one knows who the Father is except the Son, and no one knows who the Son is except the Father" [Matt. 11:27]. We have learned that the Son is immutable and unchangeable, as the Father, and self-sufficient and perfect like the Father, wanting only his unbegotten character. He is an exact and identical image of the Father. It is clear that the image contains all things by which the greater likeness exists, as the Lord himself teaches, saying, (48) "My Father is greater than I" [John 14:28]. According to this, we also believe that the Son always is from the Father. "For he is the brightness of his glory

and image of the Father's *hypostasis*" [Heb. 1:3]. But no one should take the "always" as a reference to the supposition that he is unbegotten—as those who are blinded in the faculties of their minds think—for "he was" or "always" or "before the ages" are not the same thing as unbegotten (49) But whatever the thought men will be eager to form as a word, it does not explain unbegotten (as I believe that you understand thus, and I have confidence in your orthodox statement concerning all these things)—these things in no way explain the unbegotten. (50) It seems as if these names are an extension of times, because they are not able to signify worthily the divinity of the only-begotten and, as it were, his being from the beginning. Holy men, according to the ability of each, struggle to manifest the mystery and request forgiveness from their hearers by the reasonable defense of saying, ". . . As far as those things which we have attained." (51) But if these men, who say that the things known in part are destroyed, expect something beyond human ability, some greater words through lips, it is clear that "he was," "always," and "before ages"— whatever they might be, they are not the same as the unbegotten—fall far short of the desired intent. (52) Therefore the characteristic high status must be preserved for the unbegotten Father by saying that no one is the cause of his being. But the befitting honor must be assigned to the Son by ascribing to him generation without beginning from the Father. And as we anticipated, we assign to him worship, only piously and religiously stating in regard to him "he was," "always," and "before ages," not removing his divinity but ascribing his perfect likeness in all things to the image and impress of the Father, and thinking to allow to the Father alone as a characteristic property the unbegotten, which even the Savior himself said, "My Father is greater than I" [John 14:28].

(53) But in addition to this pious faith about the Father and the Son, we confess one Spirit, as the divine Scriptures teach us, the Spirit who moved the holy men of the Old Testament and the divine teachers of the Testament called new; and we also confess one only catholic and apostolic church, indestructible always, even if the whole world would wish to combat it, and victorious over every most impious revolt of the heterodox. So we are of good courage when the Master of the church establishes it, shouting, "Be confident, I have conquered the world" [John 16:33]. (54) After this, we know the resurrection of the dead of which our Lord Jesus Christ became the firstfruit, truly having borne a body, and not in appearance, from Mary the God-bearing, "at the end of the ages for the removal of sin" [Heb. 9:26], having resided in the race of men, crucified, and died. But a lessening of his divinity did not occur on account of these things; he was taken up into heaven, and he "sat at the right hand of the Majesty" [Heb. 1:3].

(55) I have noted these things in part in the letter, having thought, and said, that it is burdensome to write down each thing in detail, because these things do not escape your holy attention. These things we teach, these things

we proclaim, these are the apostolic doctrines of the church, for which we will even die. We think less of those who would force us to deny them, and even if they force us by tortures we would not be dissuaded from our hope in them. (56) Those around Arius and Achillas, who became hostile to these doctrines, and those with them who are enemies of the truth, have been expelled from the church. They became aliens to our pious teachings. As the blessed Paul said, "If anyone preaches to you contrary to that which you received, let them be accursed even if he should pretend to be an angel from heaven" [Gal. 1:9] and "If anyone teaches otherwise and does not apply himself to the sound words of our Lord Jesus Christ and his teaching which is in accord with piety, he is arrogant, knowing nothing. . . ." [1 Tim. 6:3-4]. (57) Therefore let no one of you receive them condemned and separated from the brotherhood or support their statements or writings. The cheats falsify everything; they never speak with truth. (58) They go about the cities, eager to do nothing without the pretext of friendship and in the name of peace to give and receive letters through hypocrisy and flattery, so that they may lead astray the few women deceived by them and laden with sins etc. [cf. 2 Tim. 3:6].

(59) Therefore, beloved and brothers united in soul, avoid those who dared such things against Christ, who tear Christianity to pieces in public, who strive to parade it before courts of justice, who as much as possible aroused persecution on us in peace, and who cut the very sinews of the ineffable mystery of Christ's generation. Become confederates against their crazy daring, as our fellow ministers who now annoyed have written to me against them, and have subscribed to the document. I have sent these things through my son Apion, the deacon, to you, that is, you of all Egypt and Thebais, and of Libya, Pentapolis, Syria, and even Lycia, Pamphylia, Asia, Cappadocia, and the other neighboring countries, of which in like manner I trust that by you they are received. (60) I have provided many remedies for those who have been deceived. This remedy against their spells has been found by the laity led astray by them, when they are eager to come through this to repentance, to trust in the approvals of our fellow ministers. Greet one another with the brotherhood which is with you. I pray that you are strong in the Lord, beloved, that I may profit from your devout soul.

These are the heretics condemned and separated from the church, from the presbyters Arius, Achillas, Aeithales, Sarmates, Carpones, another Arius, and from the deacons Gaius, Euzoius, Lucius, Julius, Menas, Helladius.

5

The Synodal Letter of the Council of Antioch, A.D. 325

A rescript of those items written by the Synod, which gathered at Antioch, to Alexander the bishop of Thessalonica

(1) To Alexander, holy and united in soul with us, a beloved brother and fellow minister; Hosius, Eustathius, Amphion, Bassianus, Zenobius, Piperius, Salamanes, Gregory, Magnus, Peter, Longinus, Manicius, Mocimus, Apapius, Macedonius, Paul, Bassianus, Seleucus, Sopatros, Antiochus, Macarius, Jacob, Hellanicus, Nicetas, Archelaus, Macrinus, Germanus, Anatolius, Zoilus, Cyril, Paulinus, Aetius, Moses, Eustathius, Alexander, Eirenaius, Rabbulas, Paul, Lupus, Nicomachus, Philoxenus, Maximus, Marinus, Euphantion, Tarcondimantus, Eirenicus, Peter, Pegasius, Eupsychius, Asclepius, Alpheius, Bassus, Gerontius, Hesychius, Avidius, and Terentius send greetings in the Lord.

(2) Since the catholic church in every place is one body, even if in different places there might be dwellings of congregations, just as members of the whole body, it is suitable to your love to know the things moved and done by me and our holy brothers, fellow ministers united in soul with us. Thus you also, just as if present in the common spirit with us, could speak and act in common about those things determined and done by us soundly and according to the law of the church. (3) For after I came into the church of the Antiochenes and saw the church in much disorder with weeds because of the teaching of some and in discord, it seemed to me to be good that such conditions be thrown off and repelled not by me alone; rather, it seemed necessary to urge the involvement of those united in soul with us and fellow ministers, those especially near the matter, which is pressing and urgent to our brothers— those from Palestine and Arabia, and from Phoenicia and Coelesyria, from Cilicia and some from Cappadocia—so that after we examined and reviewed matters with common reasoning we could finally determine the matters of the church, for the city is peopled by many and just individuals. (4) Therefore, when God's grace brought us together in the diocese in Antioch, we examined and took trouble over matters common, helpful, and useful to the church of

God. We discovered especially much disorder, because in many cases the law of the church had been little esteemed and scorned, and in the interval the canons were entirely put to an end by individuals of the world. (5) Since a synod of bishops was hindered from being assembled in places of these regions, it seemed good and just that that which is of the highest priority of all, exceeding all others, be examined, rather than the entire mystery of faith in us. I mean the thing which concerns the Savior of us all, the "Son of the living God" [Matt. 16:16]. (6) Since our brother and fellow minister, the honored and beloved Alexander, bishop of Alexandria, had excommunicated from the church some of his presbyters, those around Arius, because of the blasphemy they incited against our Savior, although those presbyters were able to lead into error some individuals by their impious teaching— because of this it seemed good to the holy synod that this matter be examined just so when the major item of the mysteries was resolved, as far as it was in our power, and then all the remaining matters could be examined individually in turn. (7) And then, assembled in one place, with some erudite brothers present, we spoke at length about the faith of the church, which we had been taught by the Scriptures and apostles and which had been received from the fathers. We brought into the discussion the actions of Alexander, bishop of Alexandria, against those with Arius, so that if some individuals appeared ruined by the teaching opposite to these actions they might become estranged from the church. Thus they would not be able, by remaining within the church, to seduce some of the simpler persons.

(8) Therefore the faith put forth by spiritual men, who do not think it is just to live or reflect according to the flesh but who were trained in the Spirit by the holy writings of divinely inspired books, is as follows: to believe in one God, Father all-sovereign, incomprehensible, immutable, and unchangeable, provider and guide of all, just, good, maker of heaven and earth and all that is in them, Lord of the Law and Prophets and of the New Covenant; and (9) in one Lord Jesus, only-begotten Son, not begotten from nothing but from the Father, not as made but as properly an offspring, begotten ineffably and indescribably, wherefore only the Father who begot and the Son who was begotten know; for no one knows the Father except the Son, or the Son except the Father [cf. Matt. 11:27], who always is and not at a prior time was not. (10) We learned from the holy Scriptures that he alone is the image, not clearly as if he was unbegotten from the Father, nor by adoption, for it is impious and blasphemous to say this. The Scriptures say that he was begotten properly and truly as Son, so that we believe that he is immutable and unchangeable; he was begotten, or came into existence, neither by wish nor by adoption so that he appears to be from nothing. As far as it is probable, he was begotten not—which very thing it is not right to think—according to likeness or nature or mixture of none of the things that came into existence through him. (11) For this reason it surpasses every thought or intention or reason that we

confess him begotten from the unbegotten Father, God the Word, truth, light, righteousness, Jesus Christ, Lord and Savior of all. He is the image not of the will or of any other thing but of the *hypostasis* of the Father himself. This Son, God the Word, both brought forth in flesh from Mary the God-bearing and made flesh, suffered, died, rose from the dead, ascended into heaven, and sits on the right hand of the Majesty of the highest, coming to judge living and dead. (12) And still the Holy Scriptures teach us to believe as our Savior one Spirit, one catholic church, the resurrection of the dead, and a judgment of repayment as an individual did good or bad in the flesh, anathematizing those who say or think or proclaim that the Son of God is a creature or originated or made and not truly an offspring, or that there was once when he was not. For we believe that he was and is, and that he is light. (13) And besides we anathematize those who suppose that he is immutable by the self-act of his will, just as those who derive his generation from nothing and state that he is not immutable by nature as the Father. In all respects he is the image of the Father; thus, and especially in this regard, our Savior has been proclaimed the Father's image.

(14) Therefore this faith was set forth, and all the holy synod agreed and confessed that this is apostolic and saving teaching. All our fellow ministers thought the same thing concerning these matters. Only Theodotus of the church of the Laodiceans, and Narcissus from Neronias and Eusebius of Caesarea in Palestine, as individuals forgetting the Holy Scriptures and apostolic teachings, by various turns attempted to escape notice and conceal their errors by untrue, probable arguments, so that they appeared as persons introducing teachings opposite to these. From the works they were asked about, and that they asked about in turn, they were proved to be of the same opinion as those with Arius and to think opposite to the things mentioned previously. Thus, since they were hardened on such a matter, did not respect the holy synod which rejected their views, and acted shamefully, we all, the fellow ministers in the synod, judge not to commune with them and that they are not worthy of communion because of their faith, which is alien to the catholic church. And so that you should know, we write to you that you also guard from communion with them, from writing to them, or from receiving from them letters of communion. (15) Also know that because of the considerable brotherly love of the synod, we have given them a place for repentance and knowledge of the truth, the great and holy synod in Ancyra. Therefore, be eager to send these items around to all the brothers united in soul, so that they would be able to know the situation about these individuals and that there are certain individuals who have revolted from the church and are not in agreement with it. Greet all the brothers with you also from us. These brothers who are with us greet you in the Lord.

6

The Creed of the Synod of Nicaea
(June 19, 325)

The bishops who came together in Nicaea were nearly three hundred. They condemned the Arian heresy and defeated those around Arius. Moreover, they published in writing the ecclesiastical faith as proof against every heresy.

The items published in Nicaea were submitted as follows:

We believe in one God, Father, all-sovereign, maker of all things seen and unseen; and in one Lord Jesus Christ, the Son of God, begotten from the Father as only-begotten, that is, from the substance of the Father, God from God, light from light, true God from true God, begotten, not made, *homoousios* with the Father, through whom all things came into existence, the things in heaven and the things on the earth, who because of us men and our salvation came down and was incarnated, made man, suffered, and arose on the third day, ascended into heaven, comes to judge the living and the dead; and in one Holy Spirit. And those who say "there was once when he was not" or "he was not before he was begotten" or "he came into existence from nothing" or who affirm that the Son of God is of another *hypostasis* or substance, or a creature, or mutable or subject to change, such ones the catholic and apostolic church pronounces accursed and separated from the church.

7

The Canons of Nicaea, A.D. 325

(1) If anyone with a disease has been operated on by physicians or castrated by barbarians, let this individual remain in the clergy. But if anyone in good health has castrated himself, and he is numbered in the clergy, it is fitting that he cease functioning as clergy, and it is proper from this time that no such person be advanced.

And as it is clear that this was said concerning those who practice such a thing and dare to castrate themselves, thus if any have been castrated by barbarians or by their masters, but otherwise would be found worthy, the canon admits such ones into the clergy.

(2) Since many things were done by men either by necessity or by otherwise pressing matters contrary to ecclesiastical canon, so that men from a pagan life, who just now came to the faith and were catechized in a brief time, are led immediately to the spiritual bath and simultaneously with their baptism are advanced to the episcopate or presbyterate, it seemed good that in the future no such thing occur. Time is needed for the catechumen, and after baptism more examination. The apostolic document is plain, stating, "Not a new convert, lest puffed up he fall into judgment and the devil's snare" (1 Tim. 3:6).

But if with the passing of time some natural fault would be found about the person, and he would be convicted by two or three witnesses, let such a one cease to be of the clergy. And he who does contrary to these things, being insolent in a manner contrary to the great synod, will run a risk concerning his clerical status.

(3) The great synod altogether forbade any bishop, presbyter, or deacon, or anyone in the clergy, to have a housekeeper unless a mother, sister, or aunt, or only a person who escaped all suspicion.

(4) It is especially fitting that a bishop be consecrated by all the bishops in the province. But if such a thing would be difficult because of an urgent necessity or the length of the way, then after the voting occurred, both of those absent and of those who agreed through writing, three bishops brought together in the same place should ordain. But the confirmation of the events which occurred is given to the metropolitan in each province.

(5) Concerning those who have been excommunicated, either clergy or laity, by the bishops in each province, let the judgment prevail according to the canon, declaring that those cast out by some bishops are not to be admitted by others.

But let it be examined, lest they were cast out of the church by faintheartedness or rivalry or some such dislike of the bishop. Therefore, that this matter would receive a fitting examination, it seemed good that each year in each province synods meet twice, so that, when all the bishops of the province are brought together in the same place, such questions might be examined in common, and that those who had avowedly given offense to the bishop might seem to be excommunicated according to reason by all the bishops, until it would appear good that in the common assembly of bishops a more benevolent vote would be declared by them.

And let the synods meet, one before the forty days of Lent, so that when all faintheartedness is taken away a pure gift may be offered to God, the second synod around the season of autumn.

(6) Let the ancient customs prevail, those in Egypt, Libya, and Pentapolis, as the bishop of Alexandria has authority over all these places. This is also customary for the bishop in Rome. Likewise in Antioch and in the other provinces, the rights are to be saved for the churches.

But this is altogether clear that if someone would become a bishop without the wishes of the metropolitan, the great synod determines that such a person ought not to be a bishop. If two or three bishops on account of private rivalry speak against a common vote of all—it being reasonable and in accord with ecclesiastical canon—let the vote of the majority prevail.

(7) Since the customary and ancient tradition has prevailed, so that the bishop in Aelia (Jerusalem) be honored, let him have the consequence of his peculiar worth, apart from the honor of the metropolis (Caesarea).

(8) Concerning those who once named themselves Cathari but come to the catholic church, it seemed good to the holy and great synod that those appointed to ministerial office should remain in the clergy.

But before all it is fitting that they confess in writing that they will agree and follow the doctrines of the catholic and apostolic church, that is, have communion with those who are twice married and with those who have lapsed in persecution, for whom a time has been arranged and a season for reconciliation determined, so that they will follow the doctrines of the catholic church in all things. Therefore, where they alone would be found, either in villages or in cities, all who have been appointed to ministerial office will be in the clergy in the same rank in which they were found.

But if some come to the faith where there is a bishop or presbyter of the catholic church, it is clear that the bishop of the church will have the dignity of bishop, and that he who is named a bishop among those called Cathari will have the honor of presbyter, except if it would seem good to the bishop to share with him the honor of the name. But if this does not please him, he will think of a place for a country bishop or presbyter, so that he would seem altogether to be in the clergy but there would not be two bishops in the city.

(9) If any not examined have been advanced as presbyters, or examined have confessed their sins, and, although they confessed, men moved against the canon and placed hands on such persons, the canon does not admit such individuals to be clergy. For the catholic church justifies the blameless.

(10) As many as those who lapsed who were appointed to ministerial office in ignorance, or even if those who made the appointments knew, this does not prejudge the ecclesiastical canon. For when they are discovered, they are deposed.

(11) Concerning those who have transgressed without necessity or without the plundering of their property or without danger, or some such thing, which happened in the time of Licinius's tyranny, it seemed good to the synod, although they were unworthy of kindness, that there was kindness for them.

Therefore, as many as truly repent—as members of the faithful —will spend three years among the hearers, and for seven they will be prostrators. And during two years they will have communion with the people in prayers without the offering.

(12) And those who were called by grace, displayed the first stirring, and put aside military service—after these things they ran to their own vomit as dogs, since some threw away their cash, and achieved again by gifts military service—let these be prostrators for ten years after a time of three years with the hearers.

With respect to all these matters, it is fitting to examine the purpose and nature of their repentance. For as many as in fear, tears, endurance, and good works display their conversion in fact and not in outward show, these having finished the time determined as hearers suitably may commune with prayers. The bishop is allowed to resolve something even more generous concerning them. But as many as have received this indifferently and supposed that the outward show of entrance into the church is sufficient for their conversion, by all means let them complete the time.

Concerning those who depart this life, let the ancient and canonical law be preserved even now, so that if anyone might depart this life he should not be deprived of the perfect and most necessary provision.

And if he was mistaken and again obtained communion, and again he would belong with those who are alive, let him be with those who commune with prayer only. But on the whole, concerning anyone departing this life who requests to share in the eucharist, let the bishop give it after examination.

(14) Concerning those who are catechumens and have lapsed, it seemed good to the holy and great synod that they be hearers only for three years and afterward that they pray with the catechumens.

(15) Because of the considerable trouble and discords, it seemed good that the custom, devised in some regions, contrary to the canon by all means be removed, so that no bishop, presbyter, or deacon should be passed from city to city.

But if anyone after the definition of the holy and great synod should attempt any such thing, or should give himself to such a thing, he will be restored to the church to which he was appointed bishop or presbyter.

(16) As many bishops or deacons or those who belong in general in the rank of clergy who will withdraw from the church without the fear of God before their eyes and without knowledge of the ecclesiastical canon, these by no means ought to be accepted in another church. It is proper by every constraint to bring them to turn back into their own dioceses, or it is fitting that those continuing be excommunicated. But if any bishop would dare to snatch away a person who belongs to another and to appoint him to a ministerial office in his own church, when that person's bishop does not assent, from whom he, who belongs in the rank of clergy, has withdrawn, let the appointment be of no force.

(17) Since many who belong in the rank of clergy who chase greediness and have a sordid love of gain have forgotten the divine Scripture which says "He gave not his money to usury" [Ps. 15:5], and lending request a yearly interest of 12 percent, the holy and great synod thought it fit that if after this definition anyone would be found to have received 12 percent from the management of funds, or otherwise pursuing business, or requesting half as much again, or in short devising some other thing on account of shameful gain, he will be deposed from the clergy and will be estranged from the rank of clergy.

(18) It has come to the notice of the holy and great synod that in some places and cities the deacons give the eucharist to the presbyters, which is something neither canon nor custom granted, namely, that those who have no authority to offer should give the body of Christ to those who do offer.

And it has been revealed that now some of the deacons receive the eucharist even before the bishops.

Therefore, let all these things cease, and let the deacons remain within their own limits, knowing that they are attendants of the bishop and that they are less than the presbyters. According to their order, let them receive the eucharist after the presbyters, with either the bishop or the presbyter giving it to them. And let the deacons not be allowed to sit in the midst of the presbyters, for this happens against the canon and good order.

And if anyone would not wish to be obedient, even after these definitions, let him leave the diaconate.

(19) Concerning the Paulianists, who then flee for refuge to the catholic church, a definition has been declared that they are by all means to be baptized again. And if some in the previous time belonged in the clergy—if they would

seem to be without reproach and blameless, having been baptized again—let them be appointed to ministerial office by the bishop of the catholic church.

But if the examination would find them unfit, it is fitting that they are deposed.

But in the same manner the same ordinance will be guarded about deaconesses and, in short, those who belong in the rank of clergy. And we reminded ourselves of the deaconesses who belong in outward appearance; because they do not have any laying-on of hands, they belong by all means among the laity.

(20) And since there are some who kneel on the Lord's Day and in the days of Pentecost, so that there be a common observance in every diocese, it seemed good to the holy synod that prayers should be rendered to God with everyone standing.

8

Eusebius of Caesarea's Letter to His Church concerning the Synod at Nicaea

(1) From another source, beloved, you have probably learned what was worked out about the faith of the church at the great synod brought together in Nicaea. And this occurred because rumor is accustomed to outrun the accurate report of what things were done. But we have sent to you of necessity first the document dealing with the faith we presented, and then the second document, which they issued after they added to our words, so that the truth might not be otherwise related to you by hearsay. (2) Therefore our treatise, read in the presence of our emperor, the most beloved of God and declared to be good and worthy, is as follows:

(3) "As we have received from the bishops before us and in the first catechization, and when we received baptism, and as we have learned from the divine Scripture, and as we believed and taught in the office of presbyter and bishop itself, and thus now believing, we report to you our faith. It is this:

(4) "We believe in one God, Father, all-sovereign, the maker of all seen and unseen, and in one Lord Jesus Christ the Word of God, God from God, Light from Light, Life from Life, only-begotten Son, firstborn of all creation, before all ages begotten from the Father through whom all things came into existence; who was made flesh on account of our salvation, and lived among mankind, and suffered and rose on the third day and went up to the Father and will come again in glory to judge living and dead. And also we believe in one Holy Spirit. (5) Believing each of these to be and to exist, the Father truly Father, and the Son truly Son, and the Holy Spirit truly Holy Spirit, as also our Lord sending his disciples for proclamation said, 'Go and teach all nations baptizing them in the name of the Father and of the Son and of the Holy Spirit' [Matt. 28:19]. Concerning this, we affirm that this we maintain, and thus we think and so we have maintained previously, and we stand until death on this faith, anathematizing every godless heresy. (6) We have thought this from the heart and soul always, from which time we knew ourselves, and

49

now we think it and say it from truth; this we bear witness to in the presence of God all-sovereign, being able to show through proofs and to persuade you that during preceding times we believed and proclaimed thus."

(7) When we presented this faith, there was no opportunity for resistance by anyone. But our emperor, most beloved of God, himself first of all witnessed that this was most orthodox. He agreed that even he himself thought thus, and he ordered all to assent to subscribe to the teachings and to be in harmony with them, although only one word, *bomoousios*, was added, which he himself interpreted, saying that the Son might not be said to be *homoousios* according to the affections of bodies, and is from the Father neither according to division nor according to a cutting off, for the immaterial, intellectual, and incorporeal nature is unable to subsist in some corporeal affection, but it is befitting to think of such things in a divine and ineffable manner. And our emperor, most wise and pious, thought philosophically in this manner. But they, with the pretense of the addition of *homoousios*, produced this document:

(8) The faith composed in the synod:

"We believe in one God, Father, all-sovereign, maker of all things seen and unseen, and in one Lord Jesus Christ, the Son of God, begotten from the Father, that is only-begotten from the substance of the Father, God from God, Light from Light, true God from true God, begotten not made, *homoousios* with the Father, through whom all things, those in heaven and those on earth, came into existence, who on account of us men and on account of our salvation came down and was made flesh, was made man, suffered, arose on the third day, went up into heaven, is coming to judge living and dead. And in the Holy Spirit. And those who say, "There was once when he was not" and "Before he was begotten, he was not" and that "he came into existence from nothing," or those who allege that the Son of God is "from another *hypotasis* or substance" or is created or mutable or different, the catholic and apostolic church anathematizes." (9) When this document was composed by them, so that the phrases "from the substance of the Father" and "*homoousios* with the Father" were stated by them, we did not grant this to them without examination. Therefore, interrogations and responses occurred, and the discourse tested the sense of these phrases. Then, "from the substance" was confessed by them to be indicative of the Son's being from the Father, not as if he is part of the Father. (10) In this way it seemed good also to us to agree with the sense of the pious teaching suggesting that the Son is from the Father, not part of his substance. We also agreed with the sense, not even refraining from the expression *homoousios*, since the object of peace and the aim of not deviating from the true sense was before our eyes.

(11) In the same manner we accepted "having been begotten and not made," because they declared that "made" was a common designation of the other creatures who came into existence through the Son and to whom the Son has no resemblance. Thus he is not something made similar to things

which came into existence through him, but rather he happens to be of a better substance in comparison to anything made, which the divine oracles teach to have been begotten from the Father, because the method of begetting happens to be unutterable and beyond the understanding of every originated nature.

(12) Likewise, the argument "the Son is *homoousios* with the Father," when examined, is sound; not in the manner of bodies or as mortal beings—for the Son is so not according division of substance or by a cutting or according to any affection, mutation, or change of the Father's substance and power. The unbegotten nature of the Father is foreign to all these. (13) "*Homoousios* with the Father" indicates that the Son of God bears no resemblance to originated creatures but that he is alike in every way only to the Father who has begotten and that he is not from any other *hypostasis* and substance but from the Father. To this term, thus interpreted, it seemed well to assent, since we knew that there were certain learned ones of the ancients, famous bishops and writers, who employed the term *homoousios* in reference to their teaching about the Father and Son.

(14) Therefore let these things be said about the published faith to which we all agreed, not without investigation but according to the attributed senses examined in the presence of the most beloved of God, the emperor himself, and in agreement with the above-mentioned reflections. (15) We considered the anathema, published by them after the faith, to be harmless because of its prohibition against using words not in Scripture, from which nearly every confusion and anarchy of the church occurred. Since at any rate no divinely inspired Scripture has employed "from nothing" and "once he was not" and those things added afterward, it did not appear reasonable to say and teach these things. We agreed to this as something apparently good, because prior to this we were not accustomed to employing these words.

(16) Still it did not appear outrageous to anathematize "before he was begotten, he was not," for the confession of all is that the Son of God was before the generation according to the flesh. Already our emperor, the most beloved of God, affirmed in a discourse that even according to his divine generation he was before all the ages, since even before he was begotten in actuality, he was in the Father ingenerately in potentiality, since the Father is always the Father, both as King always and as Savior always, in potentiality being all things and being always in the same respect and in like manner.

(17) Beloved, these things we have transmitted to you of necessity, making clear to you the decision of our investigation and approval, and how reasonably we resisted then, even until the final hour, when accounts written differently offended us. But we accepted without strife those things not harmful, when it appeared to us, frankly scrutinizing the intention of the words, that they agreed with the things confessed by us in the faith previously published.

9

Arius's Letter to the Emperor Constantine

A LETTER OF THE PRESBYTER ARIUS AND EUZOIUS TO THE EMPEROR CONSTANTINE

To the most pious and beloved of God, lord, Emperor Constantine, from Arius and Euzoius.

(1) As Your Piety, beloved of God, ordered, Lord Emperor, we set forth our own faith, and we confess in writing before God that we and all those with us believe as it has been submitted. (2) We believe in one God, the Father, all-sovereign; and in Lord Jesus Christ his only-begotten Son who came into existence from him before all the ages, God the Word, through whom all things in the heavens and on earth came into existence, who came down and assumed flesh and suffered, rose and went up into the heavens and comes again to judge the living and dead. (3) And in the Holy Spirit and in the resurrection of the flesh and in the life of the future age and in the kingdom of heaven and in one catholic church of God reaching from one end of the earth to the other. (4) And we comprehend this faith from the holy Gospels, when the Lord says to his disciples, "Go teach all nations, baptizing them in the name of the Father and of the Son and of the Holy Spirit" [Matt. 28:19]. But if we do not thus believe these things and receive truly the Father, the Son, and the Holy Spirit, as the entire catholic church and the Scriptures teach, in which we put our belief in every regard, God is our judge both now and in the future day. (5) Therefore we exhort Your Piety, emperor most beloved of God, that we, being of the church and having the faith and mind of the church and the holy Scriptures, be united through your peacemaking and pious worship of God to our mother, clearly the church, so that, with inquiries and the useless talking which comes from inquiries removed, we and the church, having peace with one another, might all in common make the usual prayers for your peaceful and pious reign and for your entire family.

10

Athanasius's Orations against the Arians, Book 1

(1) Heresies—as many as are divorced from the truth—are conspicuous, even to themselves, by their insane contrivance. Their impiety has been obvious to all long ago. It is clear that those who invent heretical thoughts have departed from us, as the blessed John wrote that thought of such individuals never was, nor now is, with us [1 John 2:20]. Therefore, as the Savior said, "they not gathering with us, scatter" [Luke 11:23], with the devil, watching those who sleep, so that sowing their own poison of destruction they may have companions in death. But there is one final heresy, the Arian, which has gone forth as the forerunner of the Antichrist. Wily and villainous, seeing that her older sisters have plainly been identified as heresies, the Arian heresy employs the speech of the Scripture, as did her father the devil. She uses force to enter into the paradise of the church. She attempts to pass herself off as Christian, so that by the plausibility of false thinking (she possesses no reason!) she might beguile certain individuals to think ill of Christ. She has already led astray some foolish individuals, so that they have not only been corrupted in hearing, but receiving they ate just as Eve. Thus, being ignorant, they think that "the bitter is sweet" [Isa. 5:20] and declare the abominable heresy beautiful. Persuaded by you, I believed it necessary to tear apart the breastplate [Job 41:13] of this foul heresy and to point out the foul smell of her folly, so that those who are distant from her might flee her, and those deceived by her might repent, and with the eyes of their heart opened might discern that, just as darkness is not light, falsehood is not truth, the Arian heresy is not good. Those who consider the Arians Christians are in great error; they have not read the Scriptures, and they do not know Christianity and the faith in it.

(2) What have they seen in this heresy that is similar to pious faith, so that they talk nonsense, asserting that its followers speak no evil? This is just as if they should say that Caiaphas is a Christian, that they should include the traitor Judas with the apostles. It is like saying that those who asked for

Barabbas instead of the Savior did nothing wrong, and that Hymenaeus and Alexander should be commended for their fine thought, and that the apostle told lies about them [1 Tim. 1:20]. A Christian would not endure hearing these things; he would not grant that anyone who dares to say this is of sound mind. For among them Arius assumes the place of Christ, as Manes among the Manichees. In the place of Moses and the other saints, a certain Sotades was invented, at whom the Greeks laugh, and the daughters of Herodias. Arius himself has copied the weak and effeminate character of Sotades, writing the *Thalia*. He has emulated the dancing of Herodias, dancing about and jesting in his slanders against the Savior. The result is that those who fall into heresy are perverted in mind, act foolishly, and exchange the name of the Lord of glory for "the likeness of the image of mortal man" [Rom. 1:23]. Thus, instead of Christians they are called Arians and have this mark of impiety. Let them not make excuse. Nor let them, who are reproached, tell lies against those who are not as they are. They call Christians after their teachers so that they might seem to be called Christians themselves. Nor let them jest, ashamed of their reproachful name. If they are ashamed, let them hide their faces, or let them turn away from their own impiety. For never did Christians take their names from the bishops, but from the Lord on whom we rest our faith. Thus, although the holy apostles have become our teachers and have been ministers of the Savior's gospel, we do not take our names from them. We are from Christ, and we are named Christians. But since they have from others the beginning of what they regard as faith, it is fair that they have their name. They are their possession.

(3) Although we all are Christians, and are so called, Marcion, an inventor of a heresy, was long ago expelled. Those who stood fast with the expellers of Marcion remained Christians. But the followers of Marcion were no longer Christians. Thereafter they were called Marcionites. Thus Valentinus, Basilides, Manes, and Simon Magus have given their name to their followers. Some are addressed as Valentinians, Basilidians, Manichees, Simonians. Others are called Cataphrygians because of Phrygia, and Novatians because of Novatian. Thus Meletius, expelled by Peter the bishop and martyr, no longer called his followers Christians but Meletians. So after blessed Alexander had cast out Arius, those who stayed with Alexander remained Christians. Those who united with Arius bequeathed the name of the Savior to us who were with Alexander. Thereafter they are called Arians. See then, after Alexander's death, those who are in fellowship with Athanasius, who succeeded Alexander, and those with whom Athanasius is in fellowship—all have the same standard. They do not have the name of Athanasius. Athanasius does not take his name from them. Rather, as is the custom, they are all called Christians. For though we would have a succession of teachers, and become their disciples, being taught by them the things of Christ, we are nothing less than Christians and are so called. But the followers of heretics, though they would have countless

successors, nevertheless bear the name of the inventor of the heresy. Although Arius has died and many of his own have succeeded him, still they who think the same as Arius, acknowledged from Arius, are called Arians. Remarkable proof of this is that those from the Greeks even now coming into the church, putting away the superstition of idols, receive not the name of their catechists but the Savior's name, and instead of Greeks began to be called Christians. But those who go over to heretics, or as many as would turn from the church to heresy, forsake the name of Christ and thereafter are called Arians. This is because they no longer hold the faith of Christ but have become successors of Arius's madness.

(4) How can non-Christians be Christians? Rather, they are "Arianmaniacs"! How are those who have shaken off the apostolic faith part of the catholic church? They are inventors of new evils; they have abandoned the words of Holy Scripture, calling Arius's *Thalia* a new wisdom. They state this in fairness, for they are announcing a new heresy. Therefore anyone may have cause to wonder that although many individuals have written many works and the greatest number of homilies on the Old and New Testaments, a *Thalia* is discovered in none of them. It is found not among the serious Greeks but only among those who sing such things with their drink, clapping and joking so that others may laugh. The "marvelous" Arius copied nothing stately, not knowing the things of serious individuals. He stole the greatest number of things from other heresies and emulated the jests of Sotades alone. What was more fitting for him to do, wishing to dance against the Savior, than indicate in loose and dissolute songs his wretched words of impiety? As Wisdom says [Ecclus. 4:24], "A man is known from the utterance of his word." Thus from Arius's words the unmanly character of his soul and the perdition of his thought should be known. The crafty one did not escape notice but, as the serpent many times hoisting himself up and down, he nevertheless fell into the error of the Pharisees. The Pharisees, desiring to transgress the Law, pretended to study the words of the Law, wishing to deny the expected and present Lord. They were hypocrites in naming God. Blaspheming, they were refuted in saying, "Why do you, being a man, make yourself God?" [John 10:33], and you say, "I and the Father are one" [John 10:30]. Thus the base and Sotadian Arius is a hypocrite, speaking about God, introducing the style of Scripture. But on all sides he is proven the godless Arius, "denying the Son" and including him with those who are made [1 John 2:23].

(5) Therefore the beginning of Anus's *Thalia*, flippant, with its effeminate manner and melody, is as follows:

"According to the faith of God's elect, who have received God's Holy Spirit, I have learned these things from the sharers of wisdom, urbane, instructed by God, and wise in regard to all things. In their footsteps I came walking, of the same opinion, famous, having suffered many things for God's glory. Instructed by God I gained wisdom and knowledge."

The jokes crafted by him which are full of impiety and to be avoided for example, are, "God was not always a Father. When he was God alone he was not yet a Father; later he became a Father." "The Son was not always," for since all things came into being from nothing, and all existing creatures and works came into being, even the Word of God himself "came into being from nothing," and "there was once when he was not;" and "he was not before he came into being," but even he himself had a "beginning of his own creation." Arius says God was alone, and the Word and Wisdom were not yet. Then God, wishing to fashion us, made a certain one and named him Word, Wisdom, and Son, in order that through him he might fashion us. Thus he states that there are two Wisdoms, the one, the characteristic property, coexisting with God. In this Wisdom the Son came into being and was named Wisdom and Word only as a sharer in it. He says, "For Wisdom by the will of a wise God exists in Wisdom." Thus he says that there is another Word in addition to the Son in God, and the Son sharing in it is named, according to grace, Word and Son. This is a distinct arrogance of their heresy. The view that there are many powers is set forth in other writings of theirs. One of these powers is by nature peculiar to God and eternal. But Christ, on the contrary, is not a true power of God; he is one of the so-called powers, one of which, "the locust and the caterpillar" [Joel 2:25], is called not only a "power" but even a "great power." There are many such powers, and similar to the Son, David sings about them in the Psalter, "Lord of Powers" [Ps. 24:10]. In his nature, just as all the powers, the Word is mutable, and he remains good, as long as he wishes, by his own power. When he wishes, he himself is able to mutate, just as we are, since he is of a mutable nature. Therefore he says that God, foreknowing that he would be good, gave him in anticipation this glory which afterward he attained as man because of his virtue. Thus, because of his works, which God foreknew, God brought it about that he being of such a nature should come into being now.

(6) Arius dared to say, "The Word is not true God," "Even if he is declared God, he is not true God. By sharing grace, just as all the others is he declared God only in name." And since all are strangers and unlike God in substance, "in all respects the Word is alien and unlike the substance and property of the Father." He is peculiar to things that have come into being and to creatures; he is one of them. But after this, as a successor of the devil's reckless haste, Arius wrote in his *Thalia*, "The Father is invisible even to the Son, and the Word is able neither to see nor to know perfectly and accurately his Father." That which he knows and sees, he knows and sees proportionately in his own measure, just as we know in accord with our own power. Arius says that the Son not only does not know the Father accurately, for he is lacking in comprehension, but that the Son himself does not know his own substance. He adds, "The substances of the Father, the Son, and the Holy Spirit are divided in nature, estranged, detached, alien, and nonsharers in one another." He himself

said that the Word "in the likeness of glory and substance is totally different from both the Father and the Holy Spirit." These are the words this impious fellow spoke. He said that the Son is distinct in himself and that in all respects he does not share in the Father. These are parts of the fables of Arius written down in a laughable document.

(7) Who, hearing such things and the melody of the *Thalia*, does not justly hate Arius's jesting about such things as if he were on a stage? And because of his imagined naming of God and speaking about him, who does not see him as the serpent advising the woman? And who, reading his words one after another, does not see his impiety as the serpent's error into which that clever snake misled the woman? Who is not astonished at such blasphemies? As the prophet said, "heaven was astonished, and the earth shuddered at the transgression of the law" [Jer. 2:12], But the sun, angrier and not enduring the bodily insults against the common Lord of us all, which he willingly endured for us, turned away, veiling its rays. It rendered that day sunless. Will not all human nature be struck speechless at Arius's blasphemies and shut its ears and close its eyes, so that it would be able neither to hear such things nor to see him who wrote these things? But the Lord himself will justly cry out against these ones as impious and ungrateful in words which he spoke previously through the prophet Hosea, "Woe to them, because they have turned away from me. They are wretched because they sinned against me. I redeemed them, but they spoke lies against me" [Hos. 7:13]. And shortly thereafter, "And they calculated evil things against me, they turned away to nothing" [Hos. 7:15]. Turning away from him who is the Word of God, forming for themselves him who is not, they fell into nothing. This is why the ecumenical synod, not enduring Arius's impiety, cast Arius, who says these things, out of the church and anathematized him. Thereafter, Arius's heresy was accounted a greater error than other heresies because it has been called the enemy of Christ and considered the forerunner of the Antichrist. And, as I said previously, though such a judgment against impiety should be sufficient in itself to persuade all to flee from it, nevertheless certain so-called Christians, either ignorant or hypocrites, as was said before, regard the heresy as not different from the truth and consider the individuals who think these things Christians. As we are able, by asking them questions, let us uncover the heresy's villainy. Possibly thus entangled they would be silenced and flee from the heresy as from the face of a serpent.

(8) If then they think that because certain scriptural phrases are written in the *Thalia* this makes blasphemies words of praise, then they, seeing how the Jews of the present day know accurately the Law and the Prophets, should deny Christ with the Jews. Perhaps they, hearing the Manichees reading certain sections of the Gospels, will also deny with them the Law and the Prophets. If they do not know that they are troubled and babble such things, let them understand from the Scriptures that the devil, that designer of heresy, on

account of the peculiar ill smell of evil, borrows the language of Scripture so that with Scripture as a veil, sowing his own poison, he might outwit the guileless. He outwitted Eve; he shaped other heresies. Even now he persuaded Arius to speak and demean himself against other heresies, so that without notice he might introduce his own. Nevertheless, the villain did not escape. After he sinned against God's Word, immediately he was deprived of all. He has revealed to all that he was ignorant about other heresies; with no regard for the truth, he plays the hypocrite. How could he speak the truth about the Father, denying the Son who reveals him? How could he think correctly about the Spirit when he slanders the Word who equips the Spirit? Who will believe him when he speaks about the resurrection when he denies the statement "From the dead, Christ became for us the firstborn" [Col. 1:18]? And since he is ignorant about the legitimate and true begetting of the Son from the Father, will he not err about his incarnate presence? The Jews of a former time denied the Word by saying, "We have no king but Caesar" [John 19:15]. They all at once were deprived; they became bereft of a lamp's light, of a perfume's scent, of the knowledge of prophecy, and of truth itself. Now, comprehending nothing, they are like persons walking in darkness. Who ever heard such things? From where, and from whom, did those who flatter heresy and take bribes hear such things? Who instructing them in the faith said such things to them? Who said, "Leaving the worship of creation, come to worship a creature and a work?" And if they themselves now confess that they have heard such things for the first time, let them deny that this heresy is foreign and not from the fathers. Indeed, not from the fathers, but it has now been invented. It is the very thing which the blessed Paul foretold: "In the later times some will depart from the true faith, giving attention to spirits of error and teachings of demons, in the hypocrisy of liars; they have been burned up in their conscience" [1 Tim. 4:1] and "turning away from truth" [Titus 1:4].

(9) Behold, we speak freely about the religious faith on the basis of the divine Scriptures; we place it as a light on the lampstand saying, "He is by nature true Son and legitimate from the Father, peculiar to his substance, the only-begotten Wisdom and true and only Word of God. He is neither a creature nor a work, but an offspring peculiar to the Father's substance. Therefore he is true God, *homoousios* with the true Father. But as regards the other kings, to whom he said, "I said, you are gods" [Ps. 82:6], they have this grace from the Father only by partaking of the Word through the Spirit. He is the image of the Father's *hypostasis* [Heb. 1:3] and light from light, power and true image of the Father's substance. The Lord also said, "He who has seen me has seen the Father" [John 14:9]. He always was and is, and never was he not. Because the Father is everlasting, his Word and Wisdom would be everlasting. But what do they present to us from the universally censured *Thaliai* Let them first read it, copying the manner of the author, so that when they are mocked by others they might learn in what sort of disaster they are placed. Then let them explain. On

its basis, what might they say except, "God was not always Father but became Father later; the Son was not always, for not was he before he was begotten. He is not from the Father, but even he himself subsisted from nothing. He is not peculiar to the substance of the Father, for he is a creature and a work. Christ is not true God, but he was made God by participation. The Son does not accurately know the Father; the Word does not see the Father perfectly. Neither does the Word understand or know the Father. He is not the true and only Word of the Father, but he is called in name only Word and Wisdom and is called by grace Son and Power. He is not unmutable as the Father, but he is mutable by nature as are creatures. He lacks the comprehension of the perfect knowledge of the Father." The heresy is "admirable"; it does not even have plausibility, engaging in imaginations against him who is, on the grounds that he is not, and putting forth evil language instead of praiseworthy speech. If anyone who carefully examined the claims of both sides would be asked to choose the faith of one, or whose words he would judge appropriate to God— let these flatterers of impiety rather state, for him who is asked to answer, what is appropriate concerning God (for the Word was God). From this one request the entire issue will be known, what it is appropriate to say: he was or he was not, always or before coming into existence, everlasting or from where and when, true or by adoption, from participation and according to design, he is one of the originated or he is united with the Father, he is unlike the substance of the Father or he is like and peculiar to the Father, or he is a creature or through him creatures came into existence, he is the Father's Word or there is another Word beside him, and by this other word he came into existence, and by another wisdom, only by name he has been called Wisdom and Word, and has become a partaker of that Wisdom and second to it.

(10) Whose words discourse about God and show that Jesus Christ our Lord is God and Son of the Father? These words that you have disgorged or these that we have spoken and state are from the Scriptures? If the Savior is not God or Word or Son, you may, just as the Greeks and present-day Jews, say whatever things you wish. But if he is Word of the Father and true Son, and he is God from God once "over all blessed forever" [Rom. 9:5], is it not worthy to obliterate and expunge both the other words and the Arian *Thalia* as an image of evil, filled with every impiety in which anyone falling "does not know that giants perish with her and assemble at the trap of Hades" [Prov. 9:18, LXX]? They themselves know this, and as villains they hid it; they do not have the courage to speak them out, but they utter other things besides them. If they speak, they will be judged. If they are suspected, they will be hit in every direction with refutations from Scripture. Therefore as "sons of this age" who have villainously kindled the lamp from wild olive, and who feared lest it be quickly extinguished—for it says, "The light of the impious is quenched" [Job 18:5]—they hide it under the bushel of hypocrisy and utter different things. They profess the patronage of friends and the fear of Constantius, so that those

who join them through hypocrisy and promise will not see the filth of the heresy. Is not this heresy worthy of hate for this very reason? It is concealed by its own followers because it does not have freedom of speech, and it is fostered as a serpent. From what source were these words assembled by them? From whom did they obtain these things that they dared speak? They would say that no one individual is the supplier of these things. For who is there of humankind, Greek or barbarian, who confesses this one to be God, whom he dares to say is one of the creatures and "he was not before he was made"? Who is there who does not give credit to the God in whom he has placed his faith when God says, "This is my beloved Son" [Matt. 3:17], but rather declares that he is not a son but something made? Everyone will be angry at those who rave such things. Scripture does not provide them with any excuse. It has often been shown, and will be shown now, that these things are alien to the divine authors. Therefore it remains to say that indebted to the devil they rave (for he alone is the sower of these opinions). Come, let us resist him. Against him "is our struggle," though they are the agents [Eph. 6:12], so that, with the Lord's assistance, as one who customarily is overcome by refutations, they may be ashamed when they see the sower of their heresy without resource and may learn, although the time is late, that being Arians they are not Christians.

(11) Because the devil suggested it to you, you have said and think that there was once when the Son was not. It is necessary to strip off this first layer of your thinking. Tell them, O evil and impious ones, what was once when the Son was not. If you say the Father, your blasphemy is greater. It is impious to say that once he was or to signify him by the term "once." For he is always and is now, and as the Son is, he is, and he himself is the one who is and the Father of the Son. And if you say that the Son was once when he himself was not, the answer is foolish and unreasonable. For how was he and was not? In these circumstances it is necessary for you without resource to say, "There was once a time when the Word was not." Your adverb "once" signifies this by nature. Your former declaration, "The Son was not before he was begotten," is the same thing as the statement "There was once when he was not," for it signifies that there was that time and it was before the Word. What is the source of your discovery of these things? "Why did you, as the nations, snort and practice empty phrases against the Lord and against his Anointed?" [Ps. 2:1]. Nowhere have the Holy Scriptures said such things about the Savior; rather, they have used such words as "always," "everlasting," and "always coexisting with the Father." "For in the beginning was the Word and the Word was with God and the Word was God" [John 1:1]. And in the Apocalypse he says, "The one who is and who was and who comes" [Rev. 1:8]. Who would take away the eternal from "who is" and "who was"? Paul in his Letter to the Romans made a defense against the Jews, saying, "From whom as regards the flesh is Christ, who is over all, blessed forever?" [Rom. 9:5]. Reproving the Greeks, he said, "For from the foundation of the world his invisible nature, his everlasting power and deity,

are perceived being discerned in things made" [Rom. 1:20]. He himself teaches what the power of God is, saying, "Christ the power of God and the Wisdom of God" [1 Cor. 1:24]. Saying this, he does not signify the Father, as you often whispered, saying that the Father is his eternal power. This is not the case, for he said not "God himself is the power" but "His is the power." It is very clear to all that "his" is not "he," but something peculiar to him, not something foreign. Recognize the sequence of the words and "turn to the Lord" ("the Lord is the Spirit") [2 Cor. 3:16-17], and you will see that it is the Son who is signified.

(12) After he recalls about creation, he writes about the power of the Fashioner in creation, which power is the Word of God, through whom "all things came into existence" [John 1:3]. If therefore creation is sufficient of itself alone without the Son to make God known, pay attention lest you fall, thinking that creation came into existence without the Son. But it came into existence through the Son, and in him all things came together [Col. 1:17]. From necessity, he who views creation correctly sees the Word, who crafted it, and through him begins to discern the Father. If, according to the Savior, "no one knows the Father except the Son and him to whom the Son would disclose him" [Matt. 11:27], and if, when Philip said "Show us the Father" (John 14:9) he said not "See creation" but "He who has seen me has seen the Father," thus with reason Paul is accusing the Greeks of viewing the harmony and order of creation without thinking about the Word, the Maker, in it (for creatures reveal their own maker), so that through them they should discern the true God and should stop the worship of creatures—as I say, reasonably, Paul stated "his everlasting power and deity" so that he should indicate the Son [Rom. 1:20]. The holy writers say, "He who is before the ages" and "Through whom he made the ages" [Heb. 1:2]. They proclaim nothing *less* than the everlasting and eternal nature of the Son, while they signify that he is God. For Isaiah says, "The everlasting God, who prepares the ends of the earth" [Isa. 40:28]. Susanna said, "The everlasting God" [Susanna 42]. And Baruch wrote, "I cried to the everlasting in my days," and shortly thereafter, "I hoped in the everlasting for your salvation, and joys came to me from the holy one" [Bar. 4:20, 22]. The apostle, writing to the Hebrews, says, "Who being the reflection of the glory and image of his person" *[hypostasis, Heb. 1:3]*. David sings in Psalm 89, "The brilliancy of the Lord be upon us" [Ps. 90:17] and "In your light, we will see light" [Ps. 36:9]. Who then is foolish to have doubts about the eternity of the Son? For when did anyone see light without the brilliancy of the reflection, so that he may say about the Son, "There was once when he was not" or "Before he was begotten he was not"? And there is the statement to the Son in Psalm 144, "Your kingdom is a kingdom forever" [Ps. 145:13]. It is not permitted that anyone should infer that an interval occurred in which the Word did not exist. If every interval in the ages is measured, and the Word is king and maker of all ages, since an interval neither was nor occurred prior to him, it is madness to state that "there was once when the everlasting one was not" and "the Son

is from nothing." The Lord himself says, "I am the truth" [John 14:6], and he does not say, "I became the truth," but he always says, "I am": "I am the shepherd," "I am the light," "Do you not call me Lord and teacher? You call me well, for I am" [John 10:4; 8:12; 13:13]. Who, hearing such a phrase from God and Wisdom and Word of the Father, speaking about himself, still has doubts about the truth and will not immediately believe that in the expression "I am" is indicated that the Son is everlasting and without beginning before every age?

(13) Therefore, it is obvious from the above that the Scriptures were shown to be speaking about the everlasting nature of the Son. Those things which the Arians utter—"he was not," "before," and "when"—the same Scriptures declare about creatures. This will be clear from what follows. Moses, describing our generation, says, "And every plant of the field before its generation on the earth; and every grass of the field before its growth; for God did not moisten the earth and there was not man to work the earth" [Gen. 2:5]; and in Deuteronomy, "When the Most High divided the nations" [Deut. 32:8]. The Lord through his own person said, "If you loved me, you would rejoice, because I said, 'I go to the Father, because the Father is greater than V and now I have told you before it happened that when it happens, you will believe" [John 14:28]. Concerning creation he says through Solomon, "Before the making of the earth, and before the making of the abysses, and before the coming of the fountains of water, and before the setting of the mountains, and before all the hills, he begot me" [Prov. 8:23]. And "Before Abraham came into existence, I am" [John 8:58]. And concerning Jeremiah, "Before I formed you in the womb, I knew you" [Jer. 1:5]. And David sings in the Psalter, "O Lord, you have become our refuge in generation and generation. Before the existence of the mountains and the formation of the earth and the inhabited world, from age until age you are" [Ps. 90:1-2]. And in Daniel, Susanna cried out in a loud voice and said, "God, the eternal, who knows the secrets and who knows all things before they happen" [Susanna 42]. "Once he was not" and "before coming into existence" and "when" and such things are phrases for things originated and for creatures which have come into existence from nothing; they are foreign to the Word. If Scripture uses these for originated things and "always" for the Son, then, O enemies of God, the Son has not come into existence from nothing, he is not included among things originated, but he is the Father's image and the everlasting Word, never not being but always being as the everlasting reflection of an everlasting light. Why then do you imagine times before the Son? Or why do you blaspheme the Word as subsequent to times, through whom even the ages came into being? How did time or age subsist at all, when according to you the Word had not yet appeared through whom all things came into existence and without whom not one thing came into existence? [John 1:3]. Why, intimating time, do you not say clearly, "There was a time when the Word was not?" You omit the term

"time" to deceive the guileless, but you do not hide your own thought; even if you did, you would not escape notice. You intimate time when you say, "There was once when he was not" and "He was not before he was begotten."

(14) After these things were shown, they behave even more impudently, saying, "If there was not once when he was not, but the Son is everlasting and coexists with the Father, you say no longer that he is the Father's Son but that he is the Father's brother." Foolish and obstinate persons! If we only said that he exists everlastingly, and is not the Son, their assumed caution would be somewhat plausible. But if when we say that he is eternal we confess that he is the Son from the Father, how is he who was begotten able to be called a brother of him who has begotten? If our faith is in the Father and Son, what sort of brother is there between them? How is the Word able to be called the brother of him whose Word he is? This reply has not come from ignorant individuals, for they themselves perceive the truth. It is a Jewish "pretext" shared by those who wish, as Solomon said, "to be separated" from the truth [Prov. 18:1]. The Father and Son were not begotten from some preexisted first cause so that they might be called brothers. The Father is the origin of the Son and begat him, and the Father is Father and did not become anyone's son. The Son is Son and not a brother. If he is called the everlasting offspring of the Father, he is called so correctly. The Father's substance was not once imperfect so that what is peculiar to it should subsequently come into existence. Nor as man from man was the Son begotten so that he is later than the Father's existence, but he is God's offspring. Since he is the peculiar Son of God who always is, he exists everlastingly. It is distinctive of men to reproduce in time because of the imperfection of their nature. God's offspring is everlasting because of the continual perfection of his nature. Therefore if he is not a Son but a work that came into existence from nothing, let them prove it! Then as they are being imaginative about a work, let them call out, "There was once when he was not." Originated things, not always existing, come into existence. But if he is Son— for the Father declares this and the Scriptures shout it, and "Son" is nothing other than that begotten from the Father, and that which is begotten from the Father is his Word and Wisdom and reflection—then what is it necessary to say about those who state that "there was once when the Son was not," except that they are robbers who deprive God of his Word and they openly cry out against him that he was once without his peculiar Word and Wisdom, and the light "was once" without any gleam, and the fountain was barren and dry? Pretending to fear the term "time," because there are those who reproach them, they would say that he is "before time," but nevertheless they grant certain intervals, in which they imagine that he was not. This is nothing less than to act with extreme profanity, to declare the times and charge God with a lack of reason.

(15) If, on the contrary, they agree with us about the name of the Son, because they do not wish to be accused openly and in public, and they deny

that he is the peculiar offspring of the Father's substance, because this would suggest that he is unable to exist without the implication of parts and divisions, this is nothing less than to deny that he is the true Son and to say that he is Son only in name. Are they not greatly deceived in inferring corporeal things about the incorporeal and, because of the weakness of their peculiar nature, in denying that which is peculiar by nature to the Father? Since they do not discern how God is or the Father's origin, they deny him. Senseless ones, they measure the offspring of the Father by themselves. Those thus disposed, who think that it is not possible that there be a Son of God, are worthy of pity. Thus they must be questioned and refuted, so that they might perceive the true state of things. If according to you "the Son is from nothing and he was not before he was begotten," he has been called Son, God, and Wisdom only by participation. In such a manner are all others composed, and by sanctification they are glorified. It is necessary therefore that you tell us of what he is a partaker. All other things partake of the Spirit; according to you, then, of what is he a partaker? Of the Spirit? Rather the Spirit itself receives from the Son [cf. John 16:14], as he himself said, and it is without reason to say that the latter is sanctified by the former. Therefore he partakes of the Father. This is the only possibility, and it is necessary to say it. But what is participated then, or where does it come from? If it is external, contrived by the Father, he would be a partaker not of the Father but of an external which came into existence. No longer will he be second after the Father, because he has that other thing before him. Nor would he be called Son of the Father but of that of which he has been called Son and God. But if this is absurd and profane, when the Father says, "This is my beloved Son" [Matt. 3:17], and when the Son says, "God is his own Father," it is clear that that which is participated is not external but is from the substance of the Father. And in this also, if there would be something in addition to the substance of the Son, an equal absurdity would occur, since something would be discovered between this which is from the Father and the Son's substance—whatever it is.

(16) Therefore, because these considerations are patently absurd and contrary to truth, it is necessary to say that the Son is "from the substance of the Father," altogether peculiar to him. For it is the same thing to say that God is entirely participated and that he begets. What does "to beget" signify other than a son? Thus all things partake of the Son according to the grace of the Spirit, which comes into existence from him. From this it becomes evident that the Son himself partakes of no one and that that which is partaken from the Father is the Son. We partaking of the Son himself are said to partake of God. This is what Peter said: "That you might become partners of a divine nature" [2 Pet. 1:4]; and as the apostle also says, "Do you not know that you are the temple of God?" [1 Cor. 3:16] and "We are the temple of the living God" [2 Cor. 6:16]. Seeing the Son, we behold the Father. For the thought and comprehension of the Son are knowledge about the Father, because he is his

peculiar offspring from his substance. And just as no one of you would say that "being partaken" is an affection and a division of God's substance (for it has been shown and confessed that God is partaken, and being partaken is identical to beget), thus the offspring is neither an affection nor a division of that blessed substance. It is not absurd that God have a Son, the offspring of his peculiar substance. When we speak of Son and offspring we signify neither affection nor division of God's substance, but rather as perceiving the genuine, true, and only begotten of God, we thus believe. Since it has been said and shown that the Son is the offspring from the Father's substance, it would be doubtful to no one, but rather would be clear, that he is the Wisdom and Word of the Father, in whom and through whom he creates and makes all things. And this is his reflection, in whom he enlightens all things and is disclosed to whom he wishes. This is his character and image, in whom he is contemplated and known. Therefore both "he himself and the Father are one" [John 10:30]. He who sees him also sees the Father. This is the Christ, in whom all things are redeemed, and he again works a new creation [2 Cor. 5:17]. And since the Son is such a one, it is not fitting—it is even exceedingly dangerous—to say that he is "a work from nothing" or that "he was not before he was begotten." He who speaks thus about that which is peculiar to the Father's substance already blasphemes against the Father himself, because he thinks such things about the Father which he in error imagines about the offspring from him.

The above is enough to overthrow the Arian heresy. Nevertheless, from what follows someone might observe its heterodoxy. If God is maker and creator, and creates works through his Son, and it is not possible otherwise to view things originated other than originated through the Word—since God is the maker—how is it not blasphemous to say that his fashioning Word and Wisdom "once were not"? It is the same thing as saying that God is not maker, or that he does not have his peculiar fashioning Word within him, but that the one by whom he fashions is external, a stranger and unlike in substance. Then let them tell us, or rather let them see from this, their impiety, saying, "There was once when he was not" and "He was not before he was begotten." If the Word is not everlastingly with the Father, the Triad is not everlasting, but a monad was first, and later by addition it became a Triad, and according to them, as time went on, the knowledge of the teaching about God increased and was solidified. If the Son is not the peculiar offspring of the Father's substance but came into existence from nothing, the Triad is composed from nothing, and once there was not a Triad but a monad, and a Triad sometimes defective, sometimes completely defective, before the Son came into existence, but complete when he came into existence. Thus, thereafter, a thing originated is counted with the creator, and that which once was not is worshiped and glorified with him who always is. Of greater concern, the Triad is discovered to be unlike itself, composed of strange and foreign natures and substances. But this is nothing other than to say that the composition of the Triad is originated.

Therefore, what sort of worship of God is this which is not even like itself but is completed by the addition of time— sometimes it is not thus, sometimes it is? Probably it will again receive an addition, and this process could be without limit, since once, and at the beginning, its composition was characterized by additions. Thus it is possible that it will decrease. Obviously, things added can be taken away.

But this is not the case. May it not happen! The Triad is not originated, but there is an everlasting and one Godhead in a Triad, and there is one glory of the holy Triad. You dare to divide it into different natures. Although the Father is everlasting, you say of the Word which was seated by him that "once he was not." Although the Son was seated by the Father, you form a plan to place the Son far from the Father. The Triad is creator and fashioner, and you do not fear to reduce it to things that are from nothing. You do not feel ashamed of equating servile things with the nobility of the Triad, putting the King, the Lord of Sabaoth, with subjects. Stop confusing irreconcilable things, things which are not with him who is. You, saying these things, will bring not glory and honor to the Lord but rather ill-repute and dishonor. He who dishonors the Son dishonors the Father. If the teaching about God is now perfect in a Triad, and this is the true and only worship of God, and this is the good and the true, it was necessary that it was always thus, unless the good and the truth occurred subsequently, and the completeness of the doctrine of God is composed of additions. Therefore, necessarily, this is everlastingly so. If it is not everlastingly so, then not even in the present is it so; but at present it is, just as you suppose it was from the beginning, that is, not now a Triad. But no Christian would endure such heretics. It is peculiar to the Greeks to introduce an originated Triad and to equate it with originated things. For it is possible for originated things to accept defects and additions. But the Christian faith knows an unmoved, perfect, constant, blessed Triad. It neither adds something more to the Triad nor considers that it has a need—each of these possibilities is impious. Therefore it knows that the Triad does not mix with originated things. On guard it worships the individual oneness of its Godhead and flees the blasphemies of the Arians, and confesses and knows that the Son always is. He is everlasting as the Father, whose everlasting Word he is. Let us look at this again.

(19) If God exists and is called the fountain of wisdom and life —as by Jeremiah, "They have left me the fountain of living water" [Jer. 2:13] and again, "A throne of glory exalted, our sanctuary, the endurance of Israel, O Lord, all who have left you, let them be ashamed; let those who have withdrawn be written on the earth; because they have left the fountain of life, the Lord " [Jer. 17:12], and in Baruch, "You have left the fountain of wisdom" (Bar. 3:12)— it would follow that life and wisdom are not foreign to the substance of the fountain but peculiar to it, and that they were not once nonexistent but always were. The Son is these things, who says, "I am the life" [John 16:6] and "I

Wisdom have encamped with prudence" [Prov. 8:12]. Therefore, is not the individual impious who says, "There was once when the Son was not"? For this is the same thing as saying, "There was once when the fountain was dry, without life and wisdom." But this would not be a fountain, for that which is not begotten from itself is not a fountain. This is a load of considerable absurdity! God promises those who do his will that they will be as a fountain whose water has not failed, saying by the prophet Isaiah, "And you will be satisfied, just as your soul desires, and your bones will be fattened and it will be as a garden well watered and as a fountain which water has not failed" [Isa. 58:11]. And although God is called, and is, a fountain of wisdom, these ones dare to slander him as destitute without his own wisdom. And if the fountain is everlasting, wisdom must be everlasting, for in it all things came into existence, as David sings in the Psalter, "In Wisdom you made all things" [Ps. 104:24]. Solomon says, "God by Wisdom founded the earth, and he prepared the heavens in thoughtfulness" [Prov. 3:19]. And this Wisdom is the Word, and "through him" as John says, "all things came into existence" [John 1:3]. This Word is Christ, "for there is one God the Father, from whom are all things; we are for him, and one Lord Jesus Christ, through whom are all things, and we are through him" [1 Cor. 8:6]. If all things are through him, he himself should not be counted with the all things. He who dares to say that he, through whom are all things, is one of all the things will have the same opinion about God, from whom are all things. If anyone flees from this as absurd and distinguishes God as different from all things, it would follow that even the only-begotten Son, since he is peculiar to the Father's substance, is different from all things. If he is not one of the "all things," it is not right to say about him "There was once when he was not" and "He was not before he was begotten." Such terms are fittingly said about creatures, but the Son himself is such a one as is the Father, of whose substance he is a peculiar offspring, Word and Wisdom. This is peculiar to the Son in relation to the Father, and this shows that the Father is peculiar to the Son; so it must be stated that neither was God once Wordless nor was the Son once nonexistent. How is he a Son unless he is from him? Or how is he Word and Wisdom unless he is always peculiar to him?

(20) When was God without that which is peculiar to him? Or how is anyone able to conclude about something peculiar that it is strange and foreign? The other things such as are originated have no resemblance according to substance with their maker. They are external to him, having come into existence by his grace and will, by his Word, so that they have the potential of ceasing to be, if their maker would wish it, for this is the nature of originated things. Concerning that which is peculiar to the Father's substance (this has already been confessed to be the Son), is it not audacious and impious to say "from nothing" and that "he was not before, he was begotten" but that he came into existence subsequently and is able not to be at some time? But let the thoughtful person note how the perfection and fullness of the Father's

substance is deprived. Anyone would see more clearly the heresy's absurdity if he would consider that the Son is the "image" and "reflection of the Father," and "characteristic mark" and "truth." If when there is light, there is its image, its reflection; and when there exists a *hypostasis*, there is a complete characteristic mark of it; and when the Father exists, there is truth (the Son). Let them who measure the image and form of the deity by time ascertain how great a pit of impiety they are falling into. If the Son was not before he was begotten, truth was not always in God. But it is not right to say this. Since the Father exists, there is always in him truth, which is the Son who says, "I am the truth" [John 14:6]. Since there is a *hypostasis*, there is necessarily at once its characteristic mark and image. God's image has not externally been sketched out, but God himself has begotten it and rejoices in it, as the Son himself says, "I was that in which he rejoiced" [Prov. 8:30]. When, therefore, did the Father not see himself in his own image? Or when did he not rejoice that someone would dare to say, "The image is from nothing" and "The Father was not rejoicing before the image came into existence"? How would the maker and creator see himself in a created and originated substance? The substance of the Father must necessarily be the substance of the image. (21) Come, then. Let us look at the characteristics of the Father, that we may decide if the image is his. The Father is everlasting, immortal, powerful, Light, King, almighty God, Lord, Creator, and Maker. These characteristics are necessarily in the image, so that truly "he who has seen the Son saw the Father" [John 14:9]. And if the Son is not thus—but as the Arians think, originated and not the everlasting Son— this is not a true image of the Father, unless afterward ceasing to blush they would say that to call the Son an image is to denote not a similar substance but only his name. But, O enemies of Christ, this is not an image or a characteristic mark, for what sort of resemblance is there between things which are from nothing and the one who rendered the things which are nothing into being? How is that which is not able to be, similar to him who is, since it is inferior because once it was not and it has its own reference to things originated? The Arians, wishing him to be of such a kind, designed for themselves conclusions such as "If the Son is the Father's offspring and image and is like the Father in all things, then just as he is begotten, the Son necessarily ought to beget, and he becomes father of a son"; and again, "He who is begotten from him ought to beget, and in succession without limit, for this shows that he who was begotten is similar to him who has begotten." Inventors of evils, truly enemies of God, in order that they do not confess the Son as the image of the Father think corporeal and earthly things about the Father himself, accusing him of segments, emanations, and influxes. Therefore, if God is as a man let him become a parent as a man, so that the Son should become a father of another, and thus in succession one from another they should come into existence, so that the succession, in their opinion, might increase into a multitude of gods. But if God is not as man (for he is not), it is not necessary to attribute to him the characteristics of man. For irrational living creatures and men, after they are begun by the Fashioner, are begotten in succession from one another. A son begotten from a father, who was once a son, probably becomes the father of another, having inherited in himself from his father that by which he became himself. In these circumstances there is therefore properly neither a father nor a son. For them the paternal and filial characteristics do not remain. The son himself, being son of his father, becomes the father of his own son. This is not the case with the deity, for God is not as man. The Father is not from a father. Therefore he does not beget him who will beget a father. Nor is the Son from the emanation of the Father, nor has he been begotten from a father who was begotten. Thus he has not been begotten to beget. In the case of the deity alone, the Father is properly father and the Son properly son, and for them and them alone is it that the Father is always father and the Son always the son.

(22) Therefore let him who seeks why the Son has not begotten a son ask why the Father did not have a father. Both these questions are absurd and full of every impiety. As the Father is always father and would not ever become son, thus the Son is always son and would not ever become father. Rather, in this he is shown to be the character and image of the Father, remaining what he is and not changing himself, but having his identity from the Father. If, then, the Father changes, let also the image change, for thus are the image and reflection in relation to him who has begotten them. But if the Father is immutable and he remains what he is, the image necessarily remains what it is and will not be mutated. But he is Son from the Father. Thus he will not become something other than that which is peculiar to the Father's substance. These silly ones have foolishly contrived this point, wishing to take the image away from the Father so that they might put the Son on the same level with those originated. Arius and his supporters, placing the Son among originated ones—a view in accord with the teaching of Eusebius—and thinking that he is of a kind that such things have come into existence through him, turned away from the truth and heaped up for themselves pet words of villainy. They went around when they had just made up this heresy—and they continue even now—meeting young children in the market. They did not inquire of them something from the Holy Scriptures but, as if breaking with "the abundances of their heart" [Matt. 13:34; Luke 6:45], they say, "He who is, did he make him who is not, from that which was (not), or him who was? Therefore did he make the Son who is or who is not?" And again, "Is the unoriginated one or two ?" Is he a person of free will and not mutated by his own choice, being of a mutable nature? For he is not as a stone remaining by himself unmoved. Then they come to silly women and utter effeminate pet phrases—"Did you have a son before you gave birth? And just as you did not, thus the Son of God was not, before he was begotten." Dancing around, these dishonored individuals play with such words, and they liken God to men. Although they call themselves

Christians, "they change God's glory in the likeness of the image of corruptible man" [Rom. 1:23].

(23) It is not necessary to answer such things, since they are so foolish and silly. But so that their heresy might not appear to have some basis, it might be fitting to converse with them on such matters, especially because silly women are readily tricked by them. It is necessary for them, saying these things, to inquire of an architect if he is able to construct without material being assumed! And if he is not able, whether God was not able, without material being assumed, to make all things. And it is necessary that they ask each person if he is able to exist without a place, and if he is not able, whether even God exists in a place, so that they would be able to be shamed by their hearers. Or why if they hear that God has a Son they deny him by looking at themselves. But if they hear that he creates and makes, do they no longer oppose their human notions? It is necessary even in creation that they think human notions and furnish God with material, so that they would deny that God is creator and afterward wallow with the Manichees. But if the thought of God exceeds these things, and a person only hearing believes and knows that God is not as we are yet exists as God, and creates not as men create but as God creates, it is clear that God begets not as men beget but as God begets. God does not copy man. Rather, we men, because God rightfully and alone truly is the Father of his Son, have been named fathers of our own children. "For from him is named every family in heaven and on earth" [Eph. 3:15]. Unexamined, their statements are recognized as something thoughtful, but if anyone would reasonably examine them, they will be found to provoke much laughter and scoffing.

(24) Their initial question, being of such a kind, is foolish and ignoble. They do not indicate about whom they are inquiring so that the individual asked may answer. They simply say, "He who is," "Him who is not." Therefore who is he who is, and what are the things which are not, O Arians? Or who is the one who is once who is the one who is not? What things are said to be or not to be? For he who is, is able to make things which are not and which are and which were previously. A carpenter, goldsmith, or potter, according to his peculiar skill, works on existing and previously existing material as he makes the vessels he wishes. But the God of all, having taken the dust of the earth, which exists and came into existence by him, fashions man. The earth itself did not exist previously; he at one point in time brought it into being through his own word. Therefore, if they are inquiring about this it is clear that the creature was not before it was begotten, and that men work on existing material. Their reasoning apparently will not stand up, since things become and exist, things become and do not exist. But if they talk about God and his Word, let them finish their questioning and then ask, "Was the God who is, once Wordless? Being Light, was he lightless, or was he Father of the Word?" Or again, "Has the Father 'who is' made the Word 'who is not,' or has he always

with him the Word, a peculiar offspring of his substance?" Thus let them know that they waste their efforts and dare to deal cunningly about God and he who is from him. Who will allow them to say that God once was Wordless? Just as before, they fall into the same trap, although they were zealous to flee it and to screen it with their cunning contrivances—but were not able to do so. No one would wish to hear them disputing that God was not always the Father but later became Father, so that they might make it appear that once his Word was not. Their refutations are many. John said, "The Word was" [John 1:1]. Paul wrote, "Who being the reflection of his glory" [Heb. 1:3] and "The God who is over all blessed forever" [Rom. 9:5].

(25) It was better for them to be silent, but since they do not cease, it remains, in the light of their shameless questioning, that they should be questioned. Perhaps when they see that they are enclosed by similar absurdities they will retreat from the battle against truth. Therefore, after God is invoked for his graciousness, someone might encounter them with "The God who is, not existing, has he come into existence or is he even before he came into existence? And because he exists, did he make himself, or is he from nothing, being nothing before did he himself suddenly appear?" Such questioning is absurd—yes, absurd—and more than slander, but it is similar to their own questions. Whatever they would say is full of every impiety. If it is blasphemous, and more than impiety, to ask thus about God, it would be blasphemous to ask such things about his Word. Nevertheless, it is necessary to answer thus their irrational and stupid questions: Because God is, he is everlasting; and because the Father always is, his reflection, which is his Word, is also everlasting; again, the God who is has from himself the Word, which is. The Word did not come into existence later, not existing earlier, nor was the Father once Wordless. The audacity against the Son results in blasphemy on the Father, as if externally he designed for himself Wisdom, Word, and Son. Whichever of these terms you would mention indicates the offspring from the Father, as has been said. Their questioning does not stand up. Denying the Word, they naturally engage in irrational (wordless) questions, as if someone seeing the seen would inquire about its reflection and say, "Did he who is make that which is not, or did he make that which is?" Such a one will be seen as lacking sound reasoning and stupid, because he thinks that which is light is external to it and asks when, where, and if it has been made. Thus he who calculates such things about the Son and Father and raises such questions would be even more mad because he introduces the Word of the Father as external to him and, deceptively calling the offspring by nature a work, says, "He was not before he was begotten." Nevertheless, let them hear even to this question of theirs that the Father who is made the Son who is. "For the Word became flesh" [John 1:14]. And he made him, who is the Son of God, for the consummation of the ages also Son of man. Unless in accord with the

Samosatene, they would say that he did not even exist until he became man. In regard to their first question, this is sufficient from us.

(26) But, O Arians, recalling your own words, declare to us, "Did he who is have need of him who is not, for the fashioning of all, or did he have need of him who is?" You said that he prepared for himself as an instrument the Son out of nothing, in order that through him he might make all things. Therefore, what is better-that which needs or that which fills a need? Or do both supply those things which are lacking in the other? With such statements you show the weakness of the preparer, if he alone did not have the power to fashion all things but externally contrives for himself an instrument, just as a carpenter or shipbuilder who is unable to produce anything without an ax and saw. What is more impious than this? Why is it necessary to spend time on things so fearful, when what was said before is sufficient to show that their opinions are only an apparition? It is not proper to reply to another of their simple and silly inquiries, which they compose for silly women, except to repeat the above material: It is not right to measure the generation of God by the nature of men. Nevertheless, in order that they might judge themselves in this matter, it is good to meet them on the same basis, thus: If they ask about the parents of the Son, let them consider well the origin of the begotten child. If the parent did not have a son before he begot him, but having had him, he had him neither as external nor as foreign, but from himself and peculiar to his substance and as unchangeable image, the parent is seen in the Son and the son is beheld in the parent. If from human examples they understand that time is implied for those who beget, why should they not infer that children imply what is in accord with their parents' nature and peculiarity? But they pick from the earth, like serpents, only what is useful for poison. But inquiring of parents and saying, "You did not have a son before you begot him," they necessarily should add, "And if you had a son, then did you buy him externally as a house or some other property?" so that they might answer you, "He is not external but from me." Things external are possessions, and they pass from one person to another, but the son is from me, peculiar and similar to my substance. He did not become mine from another, but he was begotten from me; wherefore I am entirely in him, while I myself remain what I am. Thus it is that even if the parent differs in time, as a man who came into existence in time, he would have a child always coexisting, except that nature stops it and prevents it from being possible. Levi also was already in his great-grandfather's loins before he was begotten and his grandfather begot. Therefore when the man would come to this time of life, when nature supplies the power, at once, with nature unhindered, he becomes father of the son from him.

(27) If they inquired of parents about children and learned that children by nature are not external but are from parents, let them confess that the Word of God is entirely from the Father. And seeking about the time, let them state what it is that hinders God—for it is proper to expose their impious acts on the

very basis on which they scoff as they inquire—from always being Father of the Son. For it should be confessed that that which is begotten is from the Father. Thus they would entirely condemn themselves by inferring such a thing to God, just as they asked women concerning the matter of time. So let them inquire of the sun concerning its reflection, and of the fountain concerning what comes from it. They will learn that although these are offspring they are always with those from which they are. And if such parents share with their children the "by nature" and the "always," why do they conjecture that God is less than those who are originated? Do they not plainly exhibit their impiety? But if they do not dare to say this openly, and the Son is confessed to be not external but by nature an offspring from the Father, there is nothing which hinders God, for God is not as man but is greater than the sun—he is God of the sun. It is clear that the Word is from him and always coexists with the Father; through the Word the Father brought into being all things that were not. The matter itself discloses that the Son is not from nothing but is everlasting and from the Father. The question the heretics ask parents exposes their malice. They understood the issue about nature, and now they have been shamed about the issue of time.

(28) In anticipation we have said in the above material that it is not necessary to compare the generation of God with the nature of men, or to think that his Son is part of God, or that generation signifies any passion. Now we say the same thing: God is not as man. Having an unsettled nature, men beget passionately, waiting for the right time because of the weakness of their own nature. It is impossible to say this about God, for he is not composed of parts but is impassible and simple; he is without passion and indivisibly Father of the Son. Again the great proof and demonstration of this are from the Holy Scriptures. For the Word of God is his Son, and the Son is the Word of the Father and Wisdom. And Word and Wisdom is neither a creature nor a part of him, whose Word he is, nor is he an offspring according to passion. Then Scripture, uniting both terms, speaks of "Son" that it might proclaim the "by nature" and true offspring of his substance and that no one might suspect a human offspring. Again signifying his substance, it says that he is "Word," Wisdom, and reflection. From this we conclude that the generation was impassible, everlasting, and appropriate to God. Therefore what affection, what part of the Father, is the Word, Wisdom, and reflection? It is possible that even these foolish individuals can learn this. Since they inquired of women concerning the Son, let them ask men concerning the Word, so that they might learn that the Word they declare is neither their affection nor part of their mind. If such is the Word of men who are passible and divided, why do they calculate about the passions and parts of God, who is incorporeal and undivided, so that they, pretending to be discreet, may deny the true and "by nature" generation of the Son? It has been pointed out sufficiently above that the offspring from God is not an affection, and how the Word particularly has

been shown not to have been begotten according to affection. Let them hear the same things about Wisdom: God is not as man. In this regard, they should not think of him in human terms. Although men become capable of wisdom, God partakes of nothing; he is himself the Father of his own Wisdom, of which those who partake are usually called wise. This Wisdom is not an affection nor a part, but the peculiar offspring of the Father. Therefore he is always the Father, and "paternal" character does not subsequently happen to God, lest he be thought mutable. For if it is good that he is the Father, but was not always the Father, then good was not always in him.

(29) But behold, they say, "God is always a maker, and the power of fashioning does not come to him afterward." Therefore, because he is the fashioner his works are everlasting. Is it wrong to say about them, "They were not before they were begotten"? Foolish Arians, what similarity is there between Son and work that they should say the same things about the Father and fashioners. How do they remain in ignorance when in the above material such a difference between an offspring and a work has been shown? Therefore the same thing must be said: A work is external to the one who makes it, as has been said, but the Son is the peculiar offspring of the substance. Thus it is not necessary that a work always exist, for when the fashioner wishes, he works; the offspring is not subject to a wish but is a peculiar nature of substance. A person might be a maker, and may be so called, even if the works do not yet exist, but he would not be called father, nor would he be a father, if a son does not exist. If they ask why God, who is always able to make, does not make, this is the recklessness of the mad. "For who has known the mind of the Lord, or who has become his counselor" [Rom. 11:34]. Or how will something molded say to the potter, "Why did you make me thus?" [Rom. 9:20]. But so that not even some weak argument be found, let us not be silent. Let them hear that even if God always has the power to make, still things originated were not able to be everlasting, for they are from nothing and they were not before they came into existence. How are things which were not before they came into existence able to coexist with God who always is? Wherefore God, looking to their advantage, made them all when he saw that having come into existence they were able to preserve. Although he was able to send his Word from the beginning in the time of Adam, Noah, or Moses, he did not send him until the consummation of the ages— he saw that this was an advantage to every creature—and thus he made originated things, when he wished and when it was advantageous for them. But the Son, being not a work but peculiar to the Father's substance, always is. Since the Father always is, it is necessary that what is peculiar to his substance always is, and this is his Word and Wisdom. The fact that creatures are not yet in existence does not detract from the maker, for he has the power to fashion them when he wishes. But if the offspring would not always be with the Father, this is a depreciation of the perfection of

his substance. Wherefore the works were fashioned through his Word when he wished, but the Son is always the peculiar offspring of the Father's substance.

(30) These things cheer the faithful but annoy the heretical, because they see that their heresy is destroyed. Their asking "Is the Ungenerated one or two?" discloses that their thought is not accurate but suspect and full of deceit. They ask about this not for the honor of the Father but for the dishonor of the Word. Therefore should anyone, ignorant of their villainy, answer, "The Unoriginated is one," immediately they vomit forth their poison, saying, "Therefore the Son is among originated things, and we have spoken well 'He was not before he was begotten.'" They confuse and mix up all things so that they might only separate the Word from the Father and include the Fashioner of all with his works. First, in this matter, they are worthy of condemnation because they blamed the bishops gathered at Nicaea on the grounds that the bishops employed unscriptural words, although the words were not evil but destructive to their impiety. The Arians are guilty of the same accusation, speaking words not from Scripture and designing reproaches against the Lord, "not knowing either what they say or about what they maintain" [1 Tim. 1:7]. Let them ask the Greeks, to whom they listen (for it is an invention of theirs, not Scripture), so that when they hear the many meanings of the word they might learn that they are not even able to question properly about that of which they are speaking. Through them I have learned that "unoriginated" means not yet to have come into existence but being able to come into existence, as wood which has not yet become, but is able to become, a boat. And again, "unoriginated" means that which neither has come into existence nor is able ever to come into existence, for example, making the triangle quadrangular or the even number odd—for the triangle has not become, nor would it ever become, quadrangular; nor has the even number ever become odd. And again, "unoriginated" means that which exists but has not come into existence from anything, and does not have a father of its own. The villainous sophist Asterius, the advocate of the heresy, in his own little treatise added that "unoriginated" is that which has not been made but always is. Therefore it is necessary to ask in addition what meaning of "unoriginated" is intended, so that those asked might answer correctly.

(31) But if they think a good question is "Is the Unoriginated one or two?" just as unlearned individuals, they will hear that there are many such and nothing is such, for a very large number are those which are able to come into existence, and nothing is there which is not able, as has been said. But if they are asking as Asterius designed it as "that which is not a work but always is" if this were unoriginated, let them hear not once but often that Son according to this interpretation would be called unoriginated. He is neither among originated things nor a work, but he is everlasting with the Father, as has already been shown. If they often change their minds, it is only that they might speak against the Lord, "He is from nothing" and "He was not

before he was begotten." When all fails, if they wish to ask the question with another meaning of the term, namely, "being but not having been begotten from anyone, nor having a father of his own," they will hear from us that he who is thus indicated is one and unoriginated, the Father, and they will gain nothing more from hearing such things. In saying that God is unoriginated in this sense, they do not show that the Son is originated, since it is clear from the previously mentioned proofs that the Word is such a one as he who begot him. If God is unoriginated, not originated, his image is an offspring which is his Word and Wisdom. What sort of resemblance is there between the originated and the unoriginated? One must not hesitate to say the same things, because if they wish the originated thing to be similar to the unoriginated, so he who sees the one sees the other, they are close to saying that the unoriginated is also the image of creatures. Now all things become confused by them: an equaling of originated things with the unoriginated, and a destruction of the unoriginated, who is measured against works. The purpose of all this is only that they might reduce the Son into works.

(32) But I think that not even they wish to say such things, even if they are persuaded by Asterius the Sophist. For he, although zealous to plead the cause of the Arian heresy and holding that the unoriginated is one, contradicts them in saying that the Wisdom of God is unoriginated and without beginning. Here is a selection from his writings: "The blessed Paul did not say that he preached Christ, the power of God or the wisdom of God but without the article 'power of God and wisdom of God' [1 Cor. 1:24], preaching that God's peculiar power, a power innate in him and existing together with him unoriginatedly, is something other." And again after a little he wrote, "However, his everlasting power and wisdom, which the arguments of truth declare to be without beginning and unoriginated, would undoubtedly be one." Although he did not accurately discern the word of the apostle, he recognized that there were two wisdoms, but in maintaining that an unoriginated wisdom exists together with him, he says that the unoriginated is not simply one but there is also another unoriginated with him. For that which coexists does not exist with itself but with another. Therefore if they are persuaded by Asterius, let them not ask again, "Is the Unoriginated one or two?" lest they having changed their position might fight him. Or if they oppose his position, let them not rely on his treatise, lest "biting one another they might be destroyed by one another" [Gal. 5:15]. Let these things in a few words be said about their ignorance. But what could anyone say about their villainous power? Who would not justly hate them while they are mad? When they no longer had the freedom to say "from nothing" and "he was not before he was begotten," they contrived for themselves the term "unoriginated," so that declaring among the naive that the Son is originated, they might signify that "he was from nothing" and "he once was not," for by these words are suggested creatures and things originated.

(33) Therefore if they have confidence in their statements it is necessary that they stay with them and not keep recasting them. But they do not want this, recognizing at once that all is well if they propose "unoriginate" and by this term disguise the heresy. For this phrase does not have meaning in reference to the Son even if they mutter, but it does have meaning in reference to originated things. Someone might see a similar thing in "almighty" and "Lord of powers." For if the Father through his Word is master of all things and is Lord, and the Son rules the Father's kingdom and has dominion over all, as Word and image of the Father, it is very clear that the Son is not counted with all things and that God is not called almighty and Lord because of him but because of the things which came to existence through the Son, over which he is master and lord through the Word. Then "unoriginated" is indicated, not because of the Son but because of the things which came into existence through the Son; and this is fine, because God is not as originated things but through the Son is their creator and fashioner. And just as "unoriginated" is indicated with reference to originated things, so "Father" is indicative of the Son. He who names God maker, fashioner, and unoriginated sees and detects the creatures and originated things; but he, who calls God Father, immediately knows and views the Son. Some would marvel at their pertinacity, in addition to the impiety, in saying that, although the term "unoriginated" has the good intention mentioned above and is able to be named with piety, they, in accord with their own heresy, bring it forth to dishonor the Son, not having discerned that he who honors the Son honors the Father and that "he who dishonors the Son dishonors the Father" [John 5:23]. For if they cared at all about praise and honor for the Father, it was necessary —and this was better and greater— that they know and say "God the Father" rather than name him thus. As has been said before, in saying that God is "unoriginated" they are calling him, from works which come into existence, only maker and fashioner, thinking that they are able to indicate from this that the Word is a work, according to their own pleasure. But he who calls God "Father" indicates him from the Son, recognizing that since there is a Son, of necessity through the Son all originated things were created. And they who call him "unoriginated" only indicate him from his works, and they do not know the Son, just as the Greeks do not know him, but he who calls God "Father" indicates him from the Word. And knowing the Word, he knows that he is the fashioner and concludes that through him all things have come into existence.

(34) Therefore it would be more pious and true to indicate God from the Son and to call him Father than to name him from works alone and to say that he is unoriginated. For as I have said, this term individually and collectively indicates all things which have come into existence at the will of God through the Word, but "Father" is indicated and determined only by the Son. The more the Word differs from originated things, so much more would the statement that God is "Father" differ from the statement that he is

"unoriginated." For it is unscriptural and suspect inasmuch as it has variegated meaning, so that when a person is asked about it his mind is carried in many directions, but "Father" is simple, in Scripture and more true, only indicating the Son. "Unoriginated" was discovered by the Greeks, who do not know the Son. But "Father" was known by our Lord, and he rejoiced in it. He himself, knowing whose Son he is, said, "I am in the Father and the Father is in me" [John 14:10] and "He who has seen me, has seen the Father" [John 14:9] and "I and the Father are one" (John 10:30). Nowhere does he appear to call God "unoriginated." Teaching us to pray, he did not say, "And when you pray, say 'God unoriginated'" but rather "When you pray, say, Our Father, who is in heaven" [Matt. 6:9]. He wanted the summary of our faith to have the same characteristic, having commanded that we be baptized not in the name of the unoriginated and originated or in the name of the creator and creature but "in the name of the Father and Son and Holy Spirit" [Matt. 28:19]. Thus, although included in the works, we are perfected and made sons, and using the name of the Father, we recognize from this name also the Word in the Father himself. The reasoning about the phrase "unoriginated" has been shown to be foolish, nothing more than a display.

(35) Concerning their statement whether the Word is "mutable," it is superfluous to inquire about this. It is enough that I have recorded their statements to show the audacity of their impiety. Here are the nonsensical questions they utter: Has he free will or has he not? By choice, according to free will, is he good? And is he able, if he wishes, to be mutated, being of a mutable nature? Or, as stone and wood, has he not the free choice of being moved or of inclining in each of two ways? It is not foreign to their heresy to say and think such things, for once they formed for themselves a God from nothing and a created Son, it follows that they assembled for themselves such words as are suitable to a creature. But when in a struggle with members of the church they hear from them about the true and only Word of the Father, and still dare to utter such things about him, who could imagine a more disgusting thing than this teaching? Who only hearing these things, even if he would not be able to speak against them, is not confounded and will cease listening, since he *is* a stranger among these speakers? He himself hears the new words, the very utterance of which is blasphemy. For if the Word is mutable and changeable, where then will it take its stand, and what kind of end will there be to its growth? How will the mutable be able to be like the immutable? How would he who has seen the mutable think that he has seen the immutable? In what sort of condition should the Word be so that someone will be able to see in him the Father? It is clear that not always will someone see the Father in him, because the Son is always mutated and is of a changeable nature. The Father is immutable and unchanging and always is in the same condition and is the same. But if according to their opinion the Son is mutable and not always the same, but is of an always changing nature, how is such a one able to be

the image of the Father, without the similarity of his immutability? How, in brief, is he "in the Father" when he has an ambiguous purpose? But perhaps being mutable and daily making progress, he is not yet perfect. Let the Arians' madness be gone. Let the truth shine and show that they think wrongly. How is he who is equal to God not perfect? Or how is he who is one with the Father not immutable, and his Son peculiar to his substance? Since the Father's substance is immutable, his peculiar offspring from him would be immutable. If they tell lies about the mutability of the Word, since this is so, let them learn how their reason is in danger, "for even the tree is recognized by the fruit" [Matt. 12:33] and because of this "he who has seen the Son has seen the Father" [John 14:9] and the knowledge of the Son is the knowledge of the Father.

(36) Therefore the image of the immutable God should be unchangeable, "for Jesus Christ yesterday and today and forever is the same" [Heb. 13:8]. And David in the Psalter says about him, "And you in the beginning, Lord, have laid the foundation of the earth, and the heavens are the works of your hands. They will fall into ruin, but you continue; and all as a garment will become old, and you will fold them as a garment and they will be changed. But you are the same, and your years will not cease" [Ps. 102:26-28]. The Lord himself through the prophet speaks about himself: "See me, see that I am" [Deut. 32:39] and "I do not become different" [Mal. 3:6]. It could be possible to state that what is indicated here is about the Father, but it is fitting to say this also about the Son, especially because when he became man he disclosed his identity and immutability to those who think that because of the flesh he is changed and has become something other. But the saints, or rather the Lord, are more trustworthy than the malice of the impious, for according to the above-mentioned passage of the Psalter, Scripture by means of heaven and earth declares that the nature of all originated things and of every creature is mutable and changeable. Since it excludes the Son, it shows that the Son is in no way originated; rather, Scripture teaches that he changes other things not changed himself. It speaks about this: "You are the same, and your years will not cease" [Heb. 1:12]. And this is reasonable, for originated things, being from nothing and not existing before they came into existence, because not being they came into existence, they have a changeable nature. But the Son being from the Father and peculiar to his substance is unchangeable and immutable as the Father himself. It is not right to say that from the substance of the Immutable was begotten a mutable Word and a changeable Wisdom. How is he still the Word if mutable? Or how is Wisdom a changeable thing, unless as an accident in substance? They wish it to be thus so that in any peculiar substance some grace and habit of virtue occurs accidentally. This is thus called Word and Son and Wisdom, so that it is possible to take away and to add to it. Thinking such things, they often said them. But this is not the faith of Christians. The Arians do not make clear that he is the Word and truly the Son of God or that the Wisdom is true Wisdom. How is that which is mutable and

changeable not set in one and the same condition, able to be true? The Lord says, "I am the truth" [John 14:6]. If, therefore, the Lord himself says this and discloses his immutability, and the saints, having learned this, bear witness to it, and our thoughts about God acknowledge this as pious, from where did the impious contrive these things? From their heart, as from corruption, they vomited them forth.

(37) Since they put forth divine declarations as a pretext, and in accord with their own interpretation force upon them a misreading, it is necessary to reply to them, to vindicate the passages, to show that they contain the correct belief, and to show that our opponents are thinking wrongly. They declare that it was written in the apostle, "Therefore God has exceedingly exalted him and has freely given to him a name above every name, so that in the name of Jesus every knee should bow, of things in heaven, things in the earth, and things under the earth" [Phil. 2:9-10] and in David, "On account of this, God, your God, has anointed you with the oil of joy beyond your colleagues" [Ps. 45:7]. Then they bring forth as something wise the following: "If on account of this he was exalted, and received grace and on account of this he was anointed, he received a reward of his purpose. He, having acted by purpose, is entirely of a mutable nature." Not only did Eusebius of Nicomedia and Arius dare to say these things, but they dare to write them, and their followers do not hesitate to speak them in the middle of the market, not seeing the madness of their argument. For if those things he had he received as a reward of his purpose, he would not have received them unless since he was in need. His work disclosed it then, because he had these things from virtue and improvement. With reason, on account of these things, he was called both Son and God, and is not a true Son. For that which is from someone according to nature is a true offspring, as Isaac was to Abraham, and Joseph to Jacob, and the reflection to the sun. But they who are so called from virtue and grace are individuals having a grace only by acquisition instead of by nature, and they are something other in comparison to the gift, such as men who have received the Spirit by participation, concerning whom it is said, "I begot and exalted sons, but they disregarded me" [Isa. 1:2]. Because, of course, they were not sons according to nature, when they mutated the Spirit was taken away and they were disinherited. And he receives them again when they repent. And again, God giving light, who thus gave them grace at the beginning, will call them sons.

(38) Therefore, if they speak thus with regard to the Savior, it will be pointed out that he is neither true nor God nor Son nor like the Father nor in any way has God as the Father of his being according to substance, but rather that he is of the grace given to him alone and has God, according to substance, as the creator of his being like all others. Since he is of such a kind, as they say, it will be obvious that he did not have from the beginning the name "Son" if he had it as a prize for works and progress—a progress not other than

that which he made when he became man and took the form of a slave [Phil. 2:7]. For it is then that when "having become obedient until death" [Phil. 2:8-10] it is said that he was exalted exceedingly and received the name as grace, "that at the name of Jesus every knee should bend." What was prior to this if now he has been exalted and now he began to be worshiped and now was called Son, when he became man? Obviously he himself in no way improved the flesh—rather, he himself through it was improved—if accordingly to their malice then he was exalted and called Son when he became man. Therefore, what was before this? Again it is necessary to question them, that even the result of their impiety might be observed. For if the Lord is God and Son and Word but was not these things before he became man, he was something other beside these and later shared in them from virtue, just as we said. Or it is necessary that they say something else (which very thing may it rest on their heads), namely, that he himself was not before that time but that he is completely man by nature and nothing more. But this is the mind not of the church but of the Samosatene and of contemporary Jews. Therefore, because they think Jewish thoughts, why are they not circumcised as Jews? Instead they play the part of Christianity and fight against it. If he was not, or indeed was and later was improved, how did all things come into existence through him, or how in him, unless he was perfect, did the Father take delight [Prov. 8:30]? But if now improved, how did he himself before this time rejoice in the presence of the Father? And how, if after death he received worship, is Abraham seen worshiping him in the tent and Moses in the bush [Gen. 18:2; Exod. 3:4ff.]? And as Daniel saw, "myriads of myriads and thousands of thousands worshiped him" [Dan. 7:10]? And, if now he had his improvement according to them, remembering his own glory before the world and above the world, how did the Son say, "Glorify me, O Father, with the glory which I had with you before the existence of the world" [John 17:5]? But if now he has been exalted according to them, how before this time "did he bend the heavens and come down" [Ps. 18:9] and again, "The Highest gave his voice" [Ps. 18:13]? Therefore, if even before the existence of the world the Son had glory and "was Lord of glory and the Highest" and came down from heaven and is always worshiped; then having come down he was not improved, bat rather he improved the things which needed improvement. If he has descended to effect their improvement, he did not have the title of Son and God as a reward; rather, he himself has made us sons to the Father, and deified men, having become man himself.

(39) Then, not being man, he later became God; but being God, he later became man, that instead he might deify us. Because if when he became man he was called Son and God, but prior to his becoming man, God said that the ancient peoples were "sons" and made Moses as "god" of Pharaoh [Exod. 7:1], and because Scripture says of many, "God stood in an assembly of gods" [Ps. 82:1], it is clear that he was called Son and God later than they. Therefore,

how are "all things through him" [John 1:3], or how is he "the firstborn of all creation" [Col. 1:17, 15], if he had those before him who were called sons and gods? Why do the just partakers not share in the Word? This opinion is not true; it *is* an invention of contemporary Jews. For how are any able to recognize God as Father? Adoption would not happen without the true Son, who says, "No one recognizes the Father, except the Son and him to whom the Son would disclose him" [Matt. 11:27]. And how would deification occur without the Word, and before him, although he said to their brothers the Jews, "If he said that those are gods, to whom the Word of God came" [John 10:35]? And if all—as many as were called sons and gods, either on earth or in heaven—were adopted and deified through the Word, and the Son himself is the Word, it is clear through him that they all are, and he himself before all, or rather that he himself only is true Son and he alone is true God from true God, not receiving these things as a reward for virtue or being another in addition to them, but being these things by nature according to substance. For he is the offspring of the Father's substance, so that no one doubts that according to the likeness of the immutable Father the Word is also immutable.

(40) Therefore, meanwhile, using thoughts about the Son, as the Lord himself has given them, we have countered their irrational thoughts. But it is good now to set forth the divine words, that even more the immutability of the Son, the unchangeable nature of his Father, and their folly may be shown. Therefore the apostle, writing to the Philippians, says, "Have this intention in you which is also in Christ Jesus, who being in the form of God did not think being equal to God to be a prize, but emptied himself, having taken the form of a slave, having become in the likeness of men, and having been found in form as a man, humbled himself, having become obedient to death, even death of the cross. Therefore God greatly exalted him and freely gave him a name above every name, that at the name of Jesus every knee should bow, in heaven, on earth, and below the earth, and every tongue should confess that Jesus Christ is Lord to the glory of God the Father" [Phil. 2:5-11]. What would be clearer or more demonstrable than this? For not from lesser things did he become better, but rather, being God, he took the form of a slave, and in the taking he was not improved but instead humbled himself. Therefore, where in these things is there "a reward for virtue," or what kind of improvement and advance in humiliation? For if being God he became man, and having come down from the height he is said "to be exalted," where is he exalted, being God? It is clear that since God is the highest, his Word is also the highest. Therefore, how is one who is in the Father able to be exalted more and be "like the Father in all things"? Therefore he is without need of every addition, and he is not as the Arians conjecture. If the Word has descended in order to be exalted, and these things have been written, what was the need that he humble himself in order that he should seek to receive that which he has? What sort of grace did the giver of grace receive? How did he, who is always being worshiped by his

name, receive this name for being worshiped? Before he became man, the holy writers invoked, "God, by your name save me!" [Ps. 54:1]. And again, "Some in chariots and some in horses, but we extol in the name of the Lord our God" [Ps. 20:7]. And he worshiped by the patriarchs, and concerning the angels it was written, "Let all the angels of God worship him" [Heb. 1:6].

(41) And if as David sings in the Psalter, in Psalm 71, "His name remains before the sun and before the moon into generations of generations" [Ps. 72:17, 5], how did he receive that which he always had, even before receiving it now? Or how is he exalted, being most highly exalted before his exaltation? How did he receive worship, who even before receiving it now, always is being worshiped? It is not a riddle but a divine mystery. "In the beginning was the Word and the Word was with God, and the Word was God" [John 1:1], but later, for our sake, there is this passage, "the Word became flesh" [John 1:14]. The statement "He will be highly exalted" does not indicate that the substance of the Word is exalted. He was always and is "equal to God" [Phil. 2:6], but the exaltation is of the humanity. These things were not said before, only when the Word became flesh, that it might become clear that "he was humbled" and "he will be exalted" are said about the human nature. Where there is "the humble condition," there may also be exaltation. If on account of the assumption of flesh "he was humbled" was written, it is clear that "he will be exalted" was written for the same reason. Man became of flesh, and death was in need of this. Therefore, because he was the image of the Father and because he was immortal, the Word "took the form of a slave" [Phil. 2:7] and for us as man in his flesh endured death, that thus on our behalf through death he might offer himself to the Father. Therefore also as man, on account of us and on our behalf, he is said to be highly exalted, so that in his death we all have died in Christ so that in Christ himself again we may be highly exalted, being raised from the dead and rising into heaven, "where Jesus the forerunner entered on our behalf not into antitypes of true things, but into heaven itself now to appear in the presence of God on our behalf" [Heb. 6:20; 9:24]. But if now Christ entered heaven itself on our behalf, although even before and always he is Lord and fashioner of the heavens, even on our behalf this present exaltation is written. And as he himself, hallowing all, says again to the Father, "On our behalf he hallows himself [John 17:19]—not that the Word may become holy, but that he himself in himself might hallow all of us—thus the present statement "he will highly exalt him" is to be taken, not in order that he himself might be exalted, for he is the highest, but in order that he himself on our behalf "might become righteousness" [1 Cor. 1:30] and that we might be exalted in him and enter into the gates of heaven, which he himself has again opened on our behalf. The forerunners declared, "You rulers, lift up your gates and be lifted up, everlasting doors, and the king of glory will come in" [Ps. 24:7]. Thus the gates were shut not on him who is the Lord and maker of all but on account of us. Therefore humanly, because of

that flesh which he bore, it is said about him, "Lift up the gates" and "he will come in," as if a man enters. But divinely, again it is said about him—since "the Word was God" [John 1:1]—that he is the Lord and King of glory. That such an exaltation would happen to us the Spirit proclaimed in advance in Psalm 88 saying, "And in your righteousness they will be exalted, because you are the glory of their strength" [Ps. 89:17-18]. And if the Son is righteousness, then he is not being exalted as if in need, but we are those who are being exalted in that righteousness which is he.

(42) Also the phrase "he offered himself was not written because of the Word himself. Even before he became man he was worshiped, just as we said, by angels and every creature in accord with the peculiar nature of the Father. But on account of us and on our behalf, this too was written about him. For just as man Christ died and was exalted, so as man he is said "to receive" that which as God he always had, in order that such a grace given might come even to us. Having received a body, the Word was not diminished so that he should seek "to receive" grace; rather, he deified that which he put on, and more, he offered this to the human race. Just as he was always worshiped, being the Word and "being in the form of God," thus although he is the same one having become man and called Jesus, nonetheless he has all creation under his foot and "at this name bending to him their knees," and "confessing" that the Word became flesh, and in flesh endures death, this has all occurred not to the dishonor of his death but "to the glory of God the Father." It is the Father's glory that man who came into existence and was lost should be found, and who died should be made alive and should become God's temple. As the powers in heaven, angels and archangels, always worshiped him even now they worship the Lord "in the name of Jesus," this is our grace and great exaltation that even having become man the Son of God is worshiped, and the heavenly powers will not be surprised seeing us all united in his body entering their regions. But otherwise this would not have happened, except he "being in the form of God" had taken the form of a slave and humbled himself, having yielded his body to come as far as death.

(43) Behold, what is considered by men the foolishness of God on account of the cross has become more honored than all. For our resurrection is stored in it; and no longer only Israel but all nations now, as the prophet foretold, leave their idols and recognize the true God, the Father of Christ. The delusion of demons was useless, and only the true God in the name of our Lord Jesus Christ is worshiped. But the Lord, when he came in a body and was called Jesus, was worshiped and believed to be himself the Son of God, and through him the Father was recognized. All this should make it clear, as it was said, that not the Word, regarded as Word, received such kind of grace, but we received it. Because of our relationship to his body, even we became God's temple, and now we are made sons of God, so that already the Lord is worshiped in us, and those who see "announce" as the apostle said that "truly God is in them" [1 Cor.

14:25]. John says in the Gospel, "But as many as received him, he gave them power to become children of God" [John 1:12], and in the Epistle he writes, "In this we know that he remains in you by his Spirit which he gave us" [1 John 3:24]. This also is a token of the goodness from him to us, so that we were exalted because the highly exalted Lord is in us and himself humbled himself in taking our humble body and took the form of a slave when he put on the flesh enslaved to sin. He himself had nothing from us for his improvement, for the Word of God is without want and full, but we have been improved through him. "For he is the light which lightens every man coming into the world" [John 1:9]. The Arians in vain put stress on the conjunction "wherefore" on account of the statement of Paul "Wherefore God has highly exalted him." Saying this, Paul meant not a reward of virtue or improvement of his progress but the cause of the exaltation which has happened to us. But what is this other than he who is in the form of God, son of a noble Father, who humbled himself and became a slave instead of us and for us? If the Lord had not become man, we would not, having been redeemed from sins, rise from the dead, but we would remain dead beneath the earth. We would not be exalted in heaven, but we would lie in Hades. Then the statements "he has highly exalted" and "he offered" are on our account and our behalf.

(44) Therefore I consider the meaning of the passage is of such a kind, and it is especially a meaning of the church. Nevertheless, someone might make an attempt on the passage in another way, saying the same things from a parallel approach: it does not indicate that the Word himself, regarded as the Word, is exalted (for he is, as was just said above, most high and like the Father), but on account of his incarnation the passage discloses his resurrection from the dead. Then saying, "He humbled himself until death" [Phil. 2:8-9], he immediately added, "On account of this he has highly exalted," wishing to show that even if as man he is said to have died, yet being life he was exalted at the resurrection. "For he who has gone down, he himself is also the one who has risen" [Eph. 4:10]. He went down in bodily form, but he arose because he was God himself in the body. And this again is the reason he added to this meaning the conjunction "wherefore," not as a reward for virtue or for improvement, but to indicate the reason the resurrection occurred and the reason the other men from Adam until the present have died and remained dead, and he alone perfect arose. This is the cause, which he himself foretold, that being God he became man. All other men, being only from Adam, have died, and they had death "ruling" them [Rom. 5:14]. But he "the second man, is from heaven" [1 Cor. 15:47]. "The Word became flesh" [John 1:14]. And such a man is said to be from heaven and heavenly; wherefore he was not held by death. For although he humbled himself, having agreed that his own body should come to death because it was capable of death, still he was highly exalted from the earth because he is God's Son in a body. Then the statement "Wherefore God also has highly exalted him" is the equivalent to the statement

in Acts by Peter, "whom God has raised, having loosened the bonds of death because it was not possible that he should be held by it" [Acts 2:24]. For as it was written by Paul, "Since being in the form of God, he became man and he humbled himself until death, wherefore God has also highly exalted," so it is said by Peter, "Since being God he became man, and signs and wonders proved him, to those who see, to be God, and on account of this it was not possible that he should be held by death." It is not possible for a man to be successful in this, for death belongs to men. On this account, being God, the Word became flesh, that "having been put to death in the flesh, he might make all alive by his power" [1 Pet. 3:18].

(45) Because he himself is said "to be exalted" and it is said that God "offered" him, and the heretics think that this is a lack or affection in the substance of the Word, it is necessary to state the intention of these things. He himself is said to be exalted from the "lower parts of the earth" [Eph. 4:9], because death is said to be his. Both events are said to be his, because it was his body and not another's which was exalted from the dead and taken up into heaven. And again, since the body is his and the Word is not outside it, naturally when the body is exalted he himself as man, because of the body, is said "to be exalted." If therefore he did not become man, let these things not be said about him. But if "the Word became flesh," it is necessary that as concerning a man his resurrection and exaltation be mentioned, so that his death, also mentioned, might be an atonement for the sin of men and an abolition of death, and because of him the resurrection and exaltation remain secure for us. On both counts he said, "God has highly exalted him" and "God offered him," that from this he might again show not that his Father is the one who became flesh, but that his Word is the one who became man, the one who "receives" in a human manner from the Father and "is exalted" by him, as has been said. It is clear—and no one would dispute it—that those things which the Father gives he gives through the Son. It is marvelous and truly astounding, for the Son is said "to receive" the very grace which the Son gives from the Father and the Son himself is "exalted" with the very exaltation which the Son accomplishes from the Father. He being the Son of God became himself the Son of man, and as Word he gives from the Father. All things which the Father does and gives he does and supplies through him. As the Son of man, he is said to receive in a human manner the things from him, because the body is not another's but his, a body which by nature is a receiver of grace, as has been said. He received it according to the exaltation of the man, and the exaltation was his deification. But the Word himself always had this exaltation according to the Father's deity and perfection, which are his own.

(46) Therefore with such an interpretation the writing from the apostle refutes the impious. The statement by the hymnist also has the same correct intention, which the Arians misinterpret, but the psalmist shows it as holy. He says, "God, your throne is forever and ever. A scepter of justice is the scepter

of your kingdom. Having loved justice and hated injustice, because of this, God, your God, has anointed you with the oil of joy beyond your partners" [Ps. 45:6-7]. See, O Arians, and recognize the truth there. The psalmist said that we all are "partners" of the Lord. But if he were "from nothing" and one of the originated things, he himself would be one of those who partake. But since he hymned him as God eternal, saying, "Your throne, God, is forever and ever" [Ps. 45:6-7; Heb. 1:8-9], and showed that all other things partake of him, what is it necessary to think other than that he is different from originated things, that he alone is of the Father, true Word, reflection and wisdom, of which all originated things partake and are sanctified by him in the Spirit? Therefore "he is anointed" here not that he might become God, (for he was thus even before this) and not that he might become King, (he was so eternally, ruling, being the image of God [2 Cor. 4:4; Col. 1:15], as the declaration points out) but on our behalf—again this was written. The kings of Israel became kings when they were anointed, not being kings before, as David, Hezekiah, Josiah, and the others. But the Savior, on the contrary, being God and always ruling the kingdom of the Father, himself the supplier of the Holy Spirit, nevertheless is now said to be "anointed," that again, being said as a man anointed by the Spirit, he might supply us men with the indwelling and intimacy of the Spirit, just as with the exaltation and resurrection. And the Lord himself, signifying this, said in the Gospel according to John, "I sent them into the world, and on their behalf I sanctify myself, that they also may be sanctified in the truth" [John 17:18-19]. Saying this, he showed that he is not the one sanctified but the sanctifier. He is not sanctified by another, but he sanctifies himself, that we may be sanctified in the truth. He who sanctifies himself is the Lord of sanctification. How does this happen? And what does this mean except this? "I being the Word of the Father, give the Spirit to myself, when I become man; and I sanctify myself, having become man, in him (the Spirit) that now in me— I who am the truth—all may be sanctified (for 'your Word is truth')" [John 17:17].

(47) But if on our account he sanctifies himself and does this when he became man, it is very obvious that the descent of the Spirit on him in the Jordan was a descent on us because of his bearing our body. Again, it happened not for the Word's improvement but for our sanctification, in order that we may share his anointing, and about us it may be said, "Do you not know that you are a temple of God, and the Spirit of God dwells in you?" [1 Cor. 3:16]. When the Lord, as a man, was washed in the Jordan, we were the ones washed in him and by him. And when he received the Spirit, we were the ones who became recipients of the Spirit through him. On account of this he was anointed with oil, not as Aaron or David or all the others, but in another manner beyond all his fellows, with an oil of great joy, which very thing he, interpreting to be the Spirit, says by the prophet, "The Spirit of the Lord is on me because he anointed me" [Isa. 61:1]. As the apostle said, "How God

anointed him with the Holy Spirit" [Acts 10:38]. When were these things said about him, except after he had come in the flesh when he was baptized in the Jordan and "the Spirit descended on him"? [Matt. 3:16]. The Lord himself says, "The Spirit will receive of mine" and "I send him," and to the disciples, "Receive the Holy Spirit" [John 16:14, 7; 20:22], Nevertheless, he who "as Word and reflection of the Father" supplies to others is said now to be sanctified, since he has become man and the sanctified body is his. Therefore from him we have begun to receive the anointment and seal, as John says, "And you have an anointment from the Holy One" [1 John 2:20], and the apostle, "And you have been sealed with the Holy Spirit of promise" [Eph. 1:13]. Therefore the statement is on account of us and on our behalf. From this, what sort of improvement and "reward for virtue" or—in a word—progress, in the case of our Lord, is proven? If he was not God and became God, and if he was not a king and advanced into the kingdom, your reasoning would have a vague shadow of a plausibility. But if he is God and if "the throne of his kingdom is eternal," how could God advance? Or what was lacking to him who sits on the Father's throne? And if as the Lord himself has said that the Spirit is his and that he receives from the same one, and that he sends him, then it is not the Word regarded as Word and Wisdom who is anointed with the Spirit, which is given by him, but the flesh received by him. It is the flesh anointed in him and by him so that the sanctification occurring to the Lord as man may occur to all men from him. He says, "Not from himself does the Spirit speak, but the Word is he, who gives the Spirit to the worthy." This is similar to what has been mentioned previously. The apostle has written, "He who being in the form of God, thought it not a prize to be grasped to be equal to God, but emptied himself, having received a form of a slave" [Phil. 2:6-7]. And David hymns the Lord, being eternal God and King, sent to us, having taken our mortal body. This is signified by him in the psalm: "Myrrh, oil of myrrh and cassia from your garments" [Ps. 45:8]. It is shown by Nicodemus and those around Mary when a person "came bearing a mixture of myrrh and aloes, a hundred pounds" [John 19:39] and the others those things they had prepared for the burial of the Lord's body [Luke 24:1].

(48) Therefore, what kind of advancement is there for the Immortal who took on the mortal? Or what kind of improvement is there for the Eternal who put on the transitory? Also, what kind of reward could become great to the everlasting God and King who is in the Father's bosom? Then do you not see that this also happened and was written because of us and on our behalf, in order that the Lord who became man might make us, who are mortal and transitory, immortal, and might lead us into the everlasting kingdom of heaven? Then do not blush, telling lies about divine declarations. For when our Lord Jesus Christ sojourned with us, we were improved, freed from sin, but he is the same. When he became man (for again the same thing must be said) he was not mutated, but as it has been written, "The Word of God

remains forever" [Isa. 40:8]. Of course, just as before the incarnation he, being the Word, furnished to the saints the Spirit as his own. Thus when he becomes man, he sanctifies all by the Spirit and says to his disciples, "Receive the Holy Spirit." And he gave to Moses and the other seventy [Num. 11:16], and through him David prayed to the Father saying, "Do not take your Holy Spirit from me" [Ps. [51:11]. And when he became man, he said, "I will send to you the Paraclete, the Spirit of truth" [John 25:26]. And he, being truthful, the Word of God, sent him. Therefore "Jesus Christ yesterday, today, and forever is the same" [Heb. 13:8], remaining immutable, and he is the same giving and receiving—giving as the Word of God but receiving as man. Then the one improved is not the Word, regarded as Word, for he had all things and always has them, but men, who have in him and through him the beginning of their reception. When now he is said to be anointed humanly, we are the ones anointed in him; also, when he is baptized, we are the ones baptized in him. Concerning all these things, the Savior provides light, saying to the Father, "I have given to them the glory which you gave me, that they might be one, as we are one" [John 17:22]. On our account, then, he requested glory, and "he took" and "he gave freely" and "he highly exalted" are said so that we might take and it might be given freely to us and we might be exalted in him, just as also "on our behalf he sanctifies himself, that we might be sanctified in him" [John 17:19].

(49) But if because of the connection in the psalm [Ps. 45:7] "On account of this, God, your God, has anointed you," they provide for themselves a pretext (for their own purposes) based on the phrase "on account of this," let them, unlearned of Scripture and inventors of impiety, know that "on account of this" indicates not a reward for virtue or for the action of the Word but the reason for his descent to us and for the Spirit's anointment of him on our behalf. He did not say, "On account of this he anointed you, in order that you might become God or King or Son or Word," for he was thus even before this and always is, as has been shown; rather, he said, "Since you are God and King, on account of this you have been anointed, since no one else but you could unite man with the Holy Spirit, you who are the image of the Father, according to which even from the beginning we came into existence, for yours is the Spirit." For the nature of originated things was not trustworthy for this, since angels transgressed and men misunderstood. On account of this, God was a necessity ("and the Word is God") [John 1:1] that he himself might free those who had come under a curse. If, therefore, he was "from nothing," he would not be the Christ, being one of all and himself a partaker. But because he is God, being Son of God, and is everlasting King, a reflection and likeness of the Father, on account of this, he is with reason the expected Christ, whom the Father announces to men in the revelation to his holy prophets—in order that, just as through him we came into existence, thus in him a redemption of sins might occur for all, and all things might be ruled by him. This is the reason

for his being anointed and for the incarnate presence of the Word, which the psalmist, foreseeing, proclaims, hymning the Father's kingdom, "Your throne, O God, is forever and ever; the rod of your kingdom is a rod of justice" [Ps. 45:6]. Announcing his descent to us, he says, "On account of this, God, your God, has anointed you with the oil of great joy beyond your partners" [Ps. 45:7].

What is marvelous or incredible if the Lord, giving the Spirit, is said to be anointed by the Spirit? When necessity demanded it, he did not refuse to say that he is less than the Spirit because of his human nature. For when the Jews said, "He casts out demons in Beelzebub," he answered and said to them, in order to refute their blasphemy, "But if I in the Spirit cast out demons..." [Matt. 12:24, 28]. Behold, the giver of the Spirit says now that he casts out demons in the Spirit, but this was not said for any reason other than his flesh. Since the nature of men is not sufficient of itself to cast out demons, except by the power of the Spirit, for this reason he said as man, "But in the Spirit I cast out the demons" [Matt. 12:28]. Of course, when he signified that the blasphemy against the Holy Spirit is greater than blasphemy against his humanity, he said, "Whoever would speak a word against the Son of man will have forgiveness" [Matt. 12:32]. Such were the individuals who say, "Is not this the son of the carpenter?" [Matt. 13:55]. But they blaspheme against the Holy Spirit and ascribe the works of the Word to the devil. They will have an inevitable punishment. Therefore the Lord, as a man, spoke such things to the Jews; but to the disciples, showing his deity and majesty and signifying that he was not less than the Spirit but equal, he gave the Spirit and said, "Receive the Holy Spirit" [John 20:22] and "I will send him and he will glorify me" (John 16:7, 14) and "As many things as he hears, he will speak" [John 16:13]. Therefore, just as then the Lord himself, the giver of the Spirit, does not refuse to speak, as a man "he casts out demons in the Spirit," in the same manner, being the same giver of the Spirit, he does not refuse to say, "The Spirit of the Lord is on me because he has anointed me" [Isa. 61:1], because of "his having become flesh," as John said [John 1:14] in order that it might be shown that according to both aspects we are the ones needing the grace of the Spirit in sanctification and we are the ones who are not able to cast out demons without the power of the Spirit. Through whom and from whom was it necessary that the Spirit be given other than through the Son, of whom the Spirit is also? But when were we able to receive it, except when the Word became man? The statement from the apostle shows that we would not have been redeemed and highly exalted unless he, "being in the form of God, took the form of a slave" [Phil. 2:6-7]. Thus David shows that we would not otherwise partake of the Spirit and have been sanctified unless the giver of the Spirit, the Word himself, said that he was anointed by the Spirit on our behalf. Therefore firmly we have it, since he is said to be anointed in the flesh. For since flesh has been sanctified in him and he is said as man to have received [the Spirit] on account of the flesh, we have the grace of the Spirit which follows, receiving it from his fullness [John 1:16].

(51) The statement "You have loved righteousness and you have hated injustice" [Ps. 45:7], which is added to the psalm, does not show, as you again think, that the nature of the Word is mutable, but rather it discloses his immutability. Since the nature of originated things is mutable, and some have transgressed and others have disobeyed, as has been said, and their action is unsure, often it is possible that he who now is good afterward is mutated and becomes another, so that he who now is righteous after a little while is found unrighteous. For this reason there was a need of one immutable individual so that men might have as an image and type for virtue the immutability of the righteousness of the Word. Such a thought has rationale for those who think well. Because the first man, Adam [1 Cor. 15:45], was mutated and "through sin death entered into the world" [Rom. 5:12], it was fitting that the second Adam be immutable, so that if again the serpent would attack, the guile of the serpent might be weakened, and since the Lord is immutable and unchangeable, the serpent might become feeble in its attacks against all. Just as when Adam transgressed, sin came "to all men" [Rom. 5:12], thus since the Lord became man and overturned the serpent, such strength will reach to all men, so that each of us might say, "For we are not ignorant of his thoughts" [2 Cor. 2:11]. Therefore it is reasonable that the Lord who is always by nature immutable, loving righteousness and hating injustice, is anointed and sent, that being the same and remaining himself, having taken mutable flesh, "he might condemn sin in it" [Rom. 8:3] and might furnish freedom for the ability "to fulfill now the righteousness of the law" in it [Rom. 8:3] and so to be able to say, "But we are not in the flesh but in the Spirit, if the Spirit of God dwells in us" [Rom. 8:9].

(52) In vain then and now, O Arians, have you made such a conjecture, and in vain have you attempted to excuse the words of Scripture. For the Word of God is immutable, constantly in one state, not superficially but as the Father is. How is he like the Father, unless he is thus? Or how are all things which are the Father's the Son's, unless he also has the immutability and un-changeableness of the Father? Since he is not subject to laws and is not prejudged, does he love one and hate the other, lest by fear of deprivation he would take hold of one and would be admitted in another way as also mutable? But being God and Word of the Father, he is a just judge and lover of virtue, or rather its supplier. Therefore, because he is just and holy by nature, he is said to love justice and to hate injustice, which is equivalent to saying that he loves and takes the virtuous, and turns back and hates the unjust. The divine Scriptures say the same thing about the Father: "The righteous Lord also loved righteousness" [Ps. 11:7] and "You hate all the ones who work lawlessness" [Ps. 11:5] and "He loves the gates of Zion, but the tents of Jacob are not more esteemed" [Ps. 87:2] and "He loved Jacob, but he hated Esau" [Mal. 1:2]. According to Isaiah,

there is again the voice of God saying, "I am the Lord, who loves justice and hates robbery of unrighteousness" [Isa. 61:8]. Therefore let them hear these former words as these latter, for the former were written about the image of God, or wrongly considering these as the latter, let them think of the Father as mutable. But if others say that hearing this alone is not without danger, for this reason we think well of the statement that God "loves righteousness and hates robbery of unrighteousness"—not as if he were prejudged and capable of the contrary, so to select the latter and not choose the former, for this is peculiar to originated things —and that as judge he loves and takes hold of the just and puts distance between himself and the evil. It would follow, then, to think such kinds of things about the image of God because he thus loves and hates. It is necessary that the nature of the image be of such a kind, such as is its Father, even if the Arians, as blind, would see neither the image nor anything else of divine oracles. Deprived of the thoughts of their hearts, rather than of their derangements, they flee to words of divine Scripture, where in keeping with their lack of perception they do not see the meaning; putting down their peculiar impiety as a canon, they distort all the divine oracles into conformity with it. They who speak only these things are worthy to hear nothing other than "You do err, not knowing the Scriptures nor the power of God" [Matt. 22:29]. If they would continue, it is again necessary for them to give heed and hear, "Give the things of man to man and the things of God to God" [Matt. 22:21].

(53) They say that it was written in Proverbs, "The Lord created me the beginning of his ways for his works" [Prov. 8:22], and in the Epistle to the Hebrews, the apostle says, "The more having become better than the angels, so much more he inherited a name more excellent than theirs" [Heb. 1:4], and a little later, "Wherefore, holy brothers, partakers of a heavenly calling, consider the apostle and high priest of our confession, Jesus, who is faithful to him who made him" [Heb. 3:1]. And in Acts, "Therefore let it be known to you all, all the house of Israel, that God made this Jesus, whom you have crucified, both Lord and Christ" [Acts 2:36]. Quoting these texts at every point, and mistaken about their intention, they thought on the basis of them that the Word of God was a creature and a work, one of the originated things. Thus they tricked the foolish, quoting the words as a pretense instead of the true meaning, sowing their peculiar poison of heresy. "For if they had known," they would not be impious "to the Lord of glory" [1 Cor. 2:8]; they would not misinterpret the things correctly written. If then openly declaring for Caiaphas's way, they decided on Judaizing, so that they are ignorant of the statement "Truly God will dwell on the earth" [1 Kings 8:27; Zech. 2:10], let them not scrutinize the apostolic sayings, for this is not a Jewish practice. But if, having mingled with the godless Manichees, they deny the statement "the Word became flesh" [John 1:14] and his incarnate presence, let them not bring forth the Proverbs, for this is foreign to the Manichees. But if because of an excuse and the advantage that

results to them from a love of money—and because of their apparent love of honor—they do not dare to deny "the Word became flesh," since it has been written, either let them explain correctly the words written about the incarnate presence of the Savior; or if they do deny the meaning, let them also deny that the Lord became a man. It is unseemly to confess that "the Word became flesh" and to blush at the things written concerning him, and for this reason to corrupt their meaning.

(54) It has been written, "The more having become better than the angels" [Heb. 1:4]. First it is necessary to examine this. And it is necessary, as it is fitting to do for all of divine Scripture, even here to expound faithfully the time when the apostle spoke and the person and subject about which he wrote, lest the reader, being ignorant of these and other matters, might miss the true meaning. The eunuch who was fond of learning knew this when he called to Philip, saying, "I beg you, about whom does the prophet say this, about himself or someone else?" [Acts 8:34]. He was afraid lest, having explained the reading to a person, he should stray from the correct meaning. And the disciples, wishing to learn the time of the things mentioned, called to the Lord, "Tell us when will these things be? And what is the sign of your coming?" [Matt. 24:3]. Hearing from the Savior the things about the end, they wished to learn even the time, so that they themselves should not err but might be able to teach the others. When they learned, they corrected the Thessalonians who were about to err [1 Thess. 4:13; 2 Thess. 2:1-2]. When someone has an accurate knowledge of such things he has an accurate and sound notion of the faith. But if someone misunderstands such things, he falls into heresy immediately. The followers of Hymenaeus and Alexander erred, miscalculating the time too soon, "saying that the resurrection already happened" [1 Tim. 1:20; 2 Tim. 2:17], and the Galatians erred, miscalculating the time too late, now being fond of the circumcision. Even to the present time the Jews are afflicted by a miscalculation of the person, thinking that the statement "Behold the Virgin will conceive and bear a son and they will call his name Emmanuel, which is interpreted, 'God with us'" [Isa. 7:14; Matt. 1:23] is about one of them. And they think that the statement "God will raise up for us a prophet" [Deut. 18:15] is about one of the prophets. Not learning from Philip, they suppose that the statement "as a sheep he was led to the slaughter" [Isa. 53:7] is about Isaiah or some other earlier prophet.

(55) Therefore the enemies of Christ, afflicted by such kinds of things, have fallen into abominable heresy. If they had known the person, the facts, and the time of the apostle's word, they, the foolish individuals, misunderstanding human things for the deity, would not have acted profanely. It is possible to see this if someone understands correctly the beginning of the passage. For the apostle says, "In many ways and in divers manners in the past, God, having spoken to the fathers in the prophets, in these last days has spoken to us in the Son" [Heb. 1:1], and then a little later he says, "Through himself having made

a cleansing of our sins, he sat on the right hand of the Majesty on high, the more having become better than the angels, so much the more he inherited a name more excellent than theirs" [Heb. 1:4]. The word of the apostle makes mention then concerning the time when "he spoke to us in the Son" and when a cleansing of sins occurred. But when did he speak to us in the Son, and when did "the cleansing of sins" occur? And when did he become man, but after the prophets in the last days? Still continuing with the economy in which we are concerned, speaking about the last days, logically he makes mention that not even during the former times was God silent to men, for he spoke to them "through the prophets." And since the prophets ministered and "the Law was spoken through angels" [Heb. 2:2] and the Son sojourned and "he came to minister" [Matt. 20:28], necessarily he added, "The more having become better than the angels," wishing to show that so much as the Son differs from a slave, so much the ministry of the Son became better than the ministry of slaves. Distinguishing the old and new ministry, the apostle speaks freely to the Jews, writing and saying, "The more having become better than the angels." This is the reason why throughout he did not compare and he did not say "having become a greater" or "having become more honorable," lest someone consider him and them as of the same genus. But he said "better," that the difference of the Son's nature from things begotten should be known. We have proof of these things from divine Scripture: David in the Psalter, "One day in your courts is better than a thousand" [Ps. 84:10], and Solomon proclaiming, "Receive instruction and not silver, and knowledge rather than pure gold, for wisdom is better than costly stones, and everything esteemed is not worthy of it" [Prov. 8:10-11]. For are not wisdom and the stones from the earth of another and different substance? What do heavenly courts and houses on earth have in common? Or what is the commonality of eternal and spiritual things with transitory and mortal things? Isaiah says, "These things the Lord says to the eunuchs, as many as guard my sabbaths and choose those things I wish to take hold of my covenant, 'To them I will give a named place in my house and in my walls; I will give to them an eternal name better than of sons and daughters, and it will not be cut off " [Isa. 56:4-5]. Thus there is no relationship between the Son and angels, and since there is no relationship, then "better" is said not in comparison but in contrast, on account of the difference of his nature from them. Therefore the apostle himself, interpreting "better," does not do it in any other way than to differ the Son from originated things, saying on the one hand the Son, on the other hand the slaves. The one as Son with the Father "sits on the right hand"; and the others as slaves are present and "are sent and serve" [Heb. 1:13-14].

(56) But although these things have been written thus, it is not to be inferred that the Son is originated, O Arians, but rather that he is other than originated things, peculiar to the Father, being in his bosom. From the expression here, "having become," it should not be inferred that the Son is

originated, as you think. If he simply said "having become" and was silent, there would be a case for the Arians. But since he proclaimed the "Son" through the entire passage, having shown that he is other than originated things, he did not put down bluntly the expression "having become," but he joins the word "better" to it. The writer thought that the manner of speaking is indifferent, knowing in the case of the confessed true Son that he who says "having become" is saying the same thing as "having been born" and "he is better." For "begotten" is not crucial if someone would say "he has become" or "he is made." But originated things, which are fashioned, cannot be called "begotten" except to the degree that after being made they partake of the begotten Son and thus are said to be begotten. This is not because of their peculiar nature but because of their sharing of the Son in the Spirit. The divine Scripture knows this, saying about originated things, "All things came into existence through him, and without him nothing came into existence" [John 1:3], "All things you have made in wisdom" [Ps. 104:24], and, concerning begotten sons, "To Job there were born seven sons and three daughters" [Job 1:2] and "Abraham was one hundred years when to him was born Isaac his son" [Gen. 21:5], and Moses said, "If to anyone sons are born" [cf. Deut. 21:15]. Therefore if the Son is other than originated things, alone the peculiar offspring of the Father's substance, the pretext of the Arians about "having become" is in vain. If disgraced in these things, they should be forced to say again that the words are said in comparison—and because of this, things compared are of one genus, so that the Son is of the nature of angels—they will first of all be disgraced as emulating and saying the views of Valentinus, Carpocrates, and other heretics, of whom the former said that angels are of one genus with Christ, and Carpocrates said that angels are the fashioners of the world. Perhaps because the Arians learned from them they compare the Word of God to angels.

(57) But informed against such things, they will heed the singer of hymns saying, "Who among the sons of God will be like to the Lord?" [Ps. 89:7] and "Who among the gods is like to you, O Lord?" [Exod. 15:11]. And still they will hear, if they then would learn, that comparison confessedly does happen among things of one genus, not among things of different kinds. Then no one would compare God to men or man to irrational things, or wood to stone, because of the difference of nature. God is not something to be compared, but man is compared to man, and wood to wood, and stone to stone. In such a case no one would say "better," but "rather" and "more." Thus Joseph was comely rather than his brothers, and Rachel than Leah and a star is not "better" than a star but rather differs in glory. But concerning things of different genus, when someone would compare these to one another, then "better" is said in regard to the difference, just as it was said about wisdom and stones. If therefore the apostle said "by so much more rather the Son proceeds the angels" or "by so much more he is greater," you would have a case as if the Son is compared to

angels. But now saying "he is better" and "he differs much," so much as the Son differed from slaves, the apostle shows that he is other than the nature of angels. Saying again that he is the one "who laid the foundation of all things" [Heb. 1:10], he shows that he is other than all originated things. But since he is of another substance in comparison with the nature of originated things, what sort of comparison of his substance is there, or what likeness to originated things? Again, if they would conclude such a thing, Paul will refute them saying the same things, "To whom of the angels did he say, you are my Son, this day I have begotten you? And to the angels he says, he who makes his angels spirits and his ministers a flame of fire" [Heb. 1:5, 7].

(58) Behold, "to be made" is in reference to originated things, and he says that they are things made. But in reference to the Son he does not say something made or having become, but something eternal, king, fashioner, saying, "Your throne, O God, is forever and ever" [Heb. 1:8] and "You in the beginning, Lord, laid the foundation of the earth, and the heavens are the works of your hands. They will perish, but you remain" [Heb. 1:10-11]. From which statements even they were able to understand, if they wished, that the fashioner is one thing, the things fashioned something else. God is the former, but the originated things are the latter, made out of nothing. The expression "they will perish" does not speak as if creation will be destroyed but in order that it might show the nature of originated things from their end. Things with the potential to perish, if even they would not perish because of the grace of their maker, have nevertheless come into existence from nothing, and they themselves witness that once they were not. On account of this, because they have such a nature, it is said concerning the Son "you remain," so that his eternity is shown. Since he does not have the ability to perish, as originated things have, but has continual duration, it is foreign to him to say, "He was not before he was begotten." But it is his peculiar characteristic to exist always and to remain with the Father. Therefore, if the apostle had not written these things in the Epistle to the Hebrews, even from his other letters and all Scripture they would be hindered from imagining some such thing about the Word. But since he himself has written it, and in the prior sections it has been shown that the Son is the offspring of the Father's substance, and that he is the fashioner and things are fashioned by him, and that he himself is the reflection, Word, image, and wisdom of the Father, and that originated things stand and serve below the Triad, then the Son is different in kind and substance from originated things and rather is peculiar to the Father's substance and of the same nature. For this reason the Son himself did not say, "My Father is better than I" [cf. John 14:28], lest someone suppose that he is foreign to his Father's nature, but he said "greater," not in some greatness or in time, but because of the generation from his Father. Besides, in the statement "he is greater" he showed again the particularity of his substance.

(59) And the apostle himself, in the first case, not wishing to compare the substance of the Word with originated things, said, "The more having become better than the angels," for he is not comparable; rather, they are different. But looking to the incarnate sojourn of the Word and the economy effected by him, the apostle wished to show that he is not like the previous ones, in order that the more he differed in nature from those sent ahead by him, so much the more the grace, which occurred from him and through him became better than the ministry through angels. It belongs to slaves only to request the fruits, but it belongs to the Son and Master to forgive debts and to transfer the vineyard [Matt. 21:34]. The statements by the apostle show the distinction of the Son in regard to originated things. "For this reason it is more exceedingly necessary that we give heed to the things which have been heard, lest we should slip away. For if the word spoken by angels became firm, and every transgression and disobedience received a just recompense, how will we escape having neglected so great a salvation? It was spoken by the Lord at the beginning and was confirmed for us by those who heard" [Heb. 2:1-3]. But if the Son were one of the originated things, he was not "better" than they, nor in disobedience did a greater amount of punishment get stored up because of him. Nor in the ministry of angels was there according to each angel, a greater or lesser amount of guilt in the transgressors, but the law was one, and the vengeance was one against the transgressors. But since the Word is not one of the originated things, but is the Son of the Father, for this reason the more he is better and things through him are better and superior, so much more the punishment would become worse. Then let them behold the grace which is through the Son, and let them recognize that even from his works he bears witness that he is other than originated things and that he alone is the true Son in the Father and the Father in him. The Law "was spoken through angels" and "has perfected no one," needing the sojourning of the Word, as Paul said [Heb. 7:19], but the sojourning of the Word "has perfected the work" of the Father [John 17:4]. And then "from Adam to Moses death ruled" [Rom. 5:14], but the presence of the Word "overcame death" [2 Tim. 1:10] and no longer "in Adam do we all die, but in Christ we are all made alive" [1 Cor. 15:22]. "And then from Dan to Beersheba the Law was proclaimed and in Judah alone God is known" [Ps. 76:1]. But now "into all the earth their voice has gone forth" [Ps. 19:4] and "all the earth has been filled with the knowledge about God" [Isa. 11:9] and the disciples "have made disciples of all nations" [Matt. 28:19], and now is fulfilled that which has been written, "they all will be taught of God" [Isa. 54:13]. The things shown then were a type, but now the truth has been made known and again the apostle himself after these things more clearly describes this, saying, "According to so much more Jesus became a surety of a better covenant" [Heb. 7:22] and again, "But now he has obtained a more excellent ministry by so much more that he is the mediator of a better covenant which has been established on better promises" [Heb. 8:6] and "For the Law

perfected nothing, but a better hope is introduced" [Heb. 7:19]. Again he says, "Therefore it is necessary that the patterns of things in heaven be purified with these, but the heavenly things themselves with better sacrifices" [Heb. 9:23]. Both in this verse and throughout the whole work, he attributes "better" to the Lord, the one who is better and other in comparison with originated things. Better is the sacrifice through him, better the hope in him; and better the promises through him, not great compared to small, but they are other in nature, since he who manages the economy is better than originated things.

(60) The statement "He has become a surety" indicates the security on our behalf which has occurred through him. As being Word, "he became flesh," and the "becoming" we infer to the flesh (for it is originated and happens to be a creature). This the case with "he has become," that we might expound it according to the second conclusion: for this reason he became man. Let the contentious know that they are deprived of this malice of theirs. Let them hear that Paul does not mean that his substance has become, knowing that he is the Son and Wisdom and reflection and image of the Father, but "having become" is in reference to the ministry of the covenant, according to which death, once ruling, has been abolished. Here too the ministry through him has become better in that which was impossible by the Law, while it was weak because of the flesh. "God having sent his Son in the likeness of the sinful flesh and concerning sin condemned sin in the flesh" [Rom. 8:3] deprived it of the transgression in which it was constantly held a prisoner, so that it would not receive the divine mind. Having rendered the flesh capable of the Word, he caused us to walk "no longer according to the flesh but according to the Spirit" [Rom. 8:4] and to say often, "We are not in the flesh, but in the Spirit" [Rom. 8:9] and "The Son of God came into the world not to judge the world but that he might redeem all and that the world should be saved through him" [John 3:17]. For once, as guilty, the world was judged by the Law, but now the Word received on himself the judgment, having suffered in the body on behalf of all, and he has freely given salvation to all. Seeing this, John cried out, "The law was given through Moses, grace and truth happened through Jesus Christ" [John 1:17]. Grace is better than the Law, and truth in comparison to shadow.

Therefore, as has been said, "better" could not have happened through any other than the Son, who "sits at the right hand of the Father." What does this signify other than the genuineness of the Son and that the deity of the Father is the same as the Son's. For the Son, ruling the Father's kingdom, sits on the same throne as the Father, viewing the Father's deity; "The Word is God" [John 1:1] and "He who sees the Son sees the Father" [John 14:9] and thus there is one God. Then sitting on the right, he does not put his Father on the left; but whatever is of the right hand and precious in the Father, this the Son also has and says, "All things, as many as the Father has, are mine" [John 16:15]. For this reason the Son sitting on the right sees the Father himself, though he became man. "I always saw my Lord before me, because he is on my right hand, that

I should not be shaken" [Ps. 16:8]. Again this shows that he is in the Father as the Son is in the Father and the Father in the Son [John 14:10]. For since the Father is in the right, the Son is on the right; and since the Son sits on the right, the Father is in the Son. And angels, ascending and descending, minister, but he says about the Son, "And let all angels worship him" [Heb. 1:6]. When angels minister, they say, "I have been sent to you" [Luke 1:19] and "The Lord commanded." And the Son, though he speaks in human fashion, "I have been sent" [John 17:3], and comes "to complete the work" and "to minister" [Matt. 20:28], nevertheless he says, since he is Word and image, "I am in the Father and the Father is in me" [John 14:10] and "He who has seen me has seen the Father" [John 14:9] and "the Father remaining in me does the works" [John 14:10]. For whatever someone sees in this image are the works of the Father. Thus this is sufficient to win over those who fight against the truth itself. But if, because it has been written "having become better," they do not wish to hear "having become" used of the Son as the equivalent to "have become and is," or on account of the "having become the better ministry" they do not wish to take and to understand "having become," as we said, but think from this expression that the Word is said to be originated, let them hear again briefly these things, since they have forgotten what was said.

(62) If the Son is one of the angels, let "having become" be used of him and them, and let the Son not differ at all from angels in nature. Let them be "sons," or let him be an "angel," and let them together all sit on the right hand of the Father. Or with them all let the Son stand as "a spirit in holy service sent for ministry" [Heb. 11:14], he himself in the same way as those. But if Paul distinguishes the Son from those originated, saying, "For to which of the angels did he ever say, you are my Son?" [Heb. 1:5], and this one fashions heaven and earth, but they come into existence from him, and he sits with the Father, but they ministering stood before, again to whom is it not clear that he did not speak about the substance of the Word using "having become" but about the ministry having become through him? For since he is Word, he became flesh, thus having become man "the more he became better" in ministry than the ministry which occurred through angels, so much the more a son differs from slaves and the fashioner from the things fashioned. Thus let them stop taking the "having become" in reference to the substance of the Son, for he is not one of the originated things. Let them know that it denotes ministry and an economy which came into existence. But how he became being better by nature than originated things, the things previously said disclose. Thus I consider that they should be ashamed. But if they would be contentious, in view of their most unreasonable audacity it follows that one should depart from them and set against them the similar words which have been said about the Father himself, so that ashamed they would either refrain their tongues from evil or would know how great the depth of their folly is. Therefore it has been written, "Be to me a God, a protector and a house of refuge to save me"

[Ps. 31:2] and again, "The Lord became a refuge for the poor" [Ps. 9:9]; as many such things are found in the divine Scripture. Therefore, if they say that these things are said about the Son, which is perhaps somewhat truthful, let them acknowledge that the holy writers ask him to become a help and a house of refuge, not as one originated; and now let them accept "having become," "he made," and "he created" in reference to his incarnate presence. For then he became a help and a house of refuge when "in his body on the cross he bore our sins" [1 Pet. 2:24] and said, "Come to me, all who are tired and burdened, and I will give you rest" [Matt. 11:28].

(63) But if they say that the words are spoken in reference to the Father, when even here "become" and "he has become" are written, will they the more attempt to say that God is originated? Yes, they will dare just as they discuss such things about his Word, for the sequence carries them to suppose such things even about the Father as they imagine about his Word. But may such a thing never come into the mind of any of the faithful! For neither is the Son one of the originated nor does the thing written and said thus "become" and "he became" signify a beginning of being but an aid which has occurred to those in need. God always is, and he is the same. But men subsequently have come into existence through the Word when the Father himself wished it, and God is invisible and unapproachable to originated things, and especially to men on earth. Therefore when men who are weak invoke him, when pursued they beg his aid, when harmed they pray, then the invisible One, a lover of mankind, shines forth through his kindness, which he does through his own Word and in himself, and more the divine manifestation occurs to each according to the need. It becomes strength for those who are weak, a refuge and house of salvation for those pursued. To those harmed he says, "While you speak, I will say, 'Behold I am present'" [Isa. 58:9]. Therefore whatever assistance occurs to each through the Son, this each says, that God has come into existence to himself, because assistance also comes into existence from God himself through the Word. The usage of men recognizes this, and everyone will confess that this is appropriate. Often assistance occurs from men to men— someone labored for an injured person, as Abraham for Lot [Gen. 14:13-14]; someone else opened his home to the pursued, as Obadiah to the sons of the prophets [1 Kings 18:4]; another has given rest to a stranger, as Lot the angels [Gen. 19:3]; still another supplied those in need, as Job to those who asked him [Job 29:15-16]. Therefore, if each of those who were well-affected might say, "Such a one became an assistance to me," and another might say "a refuge to me" and "to this one a supplier," when they say these things, they do not indicate the beginning of origin or the substance of those who did the good deeds but the kindness which comes to them from their benefactors. Thus whenever holy ones would say about God "he became" and "become," they indicate not some beginning of origin (for God is without beginning and unoriginated) but the salvation from him which occurred to men.

(64) But since this is thus noted, it would follow concerning the Son that whatever, and how often, would be said such expressions as "he has become" and "become," these should preserve the same meaning, so that the statements "having become better than the angels" and "he has become" should not lead to the conclusion there was some beginning of the becoming of the Word, or to the fantasy that he is originated, but Paul's expression should be understood in regard to his ministry and economy, when he became man. When "the Word became flesh and dwelled among us" [John 1:14], he came, "that he might minister and might give salvation to all" [Matt. 20:28]; then he became deliverance for us and he became life and propitiation. Then his economy on our behalf "became better than the angels," and he became a way and resurrection. And just as "Be to me a God, a protector" does not signify the beginning of the substance of God himself but, as has been said, the love of humankind, thus the expressions "Having become better than the angels," "He has become," and "So much more has Jesus become a better surety" do signify not that the substance of the Word is originated (Heaven forbid!) but the kindness which happened to us from his incarnation, although heretics might be ungrateful and contentious in regard to their impiety.

11

Gregory of Nazianzus's Third Theological Oration concerning the Son

(1) Therefore someone might say these things in demolishing the Eunomians' readiness and quickness about the Word, and also their precariousness in all affairs, but especially in discourse about God. But some reproof is nothing significant; in fact it is the easiest thing that everyone wants to do, and it is the character of a pious and intelligent man to substitute his own judgment. Then with confidence in the Holy Spirit, who is dishonored by the Eunomians but worshiped by us, let us bring into the light our own opinions about the deity— whatever they are—as a noble and opportune offspring. Not that at other times we have been silent, for on this matter we are vigorous and generous. But now even more freely we speak the truth, so that we should not, shrinking back— as it was written—be reckoned in condemnation [Heb. 10:38-39]. Since every argument is twofold, preparing its own defense and overthrowing its rival, and we earlier put forth our own position, we will attempt to overturn opposing views. We will do this in as few words as possible, so that the statements become intelligible, just as the argument they introduced and designed to deceive the more foolish and silly, and so that the remarks are not dispersed by the length of the argument, as water, not restricted by a channel, flows and spreads over a plain.

(2) The three oldest opinions about God are anarchy, government of the many, and monarchy. The first two were toyed with by the children of the Greeks—and let them so play. Anarchy is disorderly, and government of the many is seditious and thus anarchical and thus disorderly. Both result in the same thing—indiscipline—and this leads to dissolution, for indiscipline is the practice of dissolution. Monarchy is the opinion honored by us, yet a monarchy which one person does not determine, for it is possible that the one being in dispute with itself comes into a state of many. It is a monarchy composed of an equality of honor of nature, a concord of mind, identity of movement, and a convergence of things from it to the one, which is impossible for originated

nature, so that it differs in number but there is no severance in substance. Therefore, solitary from the beginning, it moved into duality and it took its place as Trinity, and this is for us the Father and Son and Holy Spirit. The Father is the begetter and producer, but I mean without passion, timelessly and incorporeally. The Son is the offspring, and the Spirit the product. I do not know how to name them, altogether removing visible things. We will not dare to mention an overflow of goodness, which a certain Greek philosopher had the audacity to say, as if a certain bowl overflows. He has spoken plainly in those words in his philosophical works about the first and second cause. Then let us not introduce the generation as involuntary, as some natural superfluity, hard to hold, least appropriate for opinions about deity. Thus stopping at our limits, we introduce the unbegotten and the begotten and the one which proceeds from the Father, as somewhere God himself, also the Word, says [John 15:26].

(3) Therefore, when did these come into existence? They are beyond "when." But if it is necessary to say something even vigorously—when the Father did. And when did the Father come into existence? There was not when he was not. And this is the case with the Son and the Holy Spirit. Ask me again, and again I will answer you. When was the Son begotten? When the Father was not begotten. When did the Spirit proceed? When the Son was not proceeding but was timelessly begotten and beyond reason. And though we are not able suggest what is beyond time, we wish to escape from a temporal image. "When," "before," "after," and "from the beginning" are not independent of time, as much as we try to force it, unless we would take the age, the internal coextensive with eternal things, not divided or measured by some movement or by the course of the sun, as time is. Then how are they not unoriginated if coeternal? Because they are from him, even if they are not after him. For the thing without a beginning is also eternal, but the eternal thing is not by all means without a beginning, as long as for its beginning it is referred to the Father. Therefore, in reference to the cause, they are not without beginning. But it is clear that the cause is not by all means older than those things of which it is the cause. The sun is not older than its light. By some means they are without beginning in reference to time, even if you scare the simpler people, for the sources of time are not under time.

(4) How then is the generation not with passion? Because it is incorporeal. For if corporeal generation is passionate, incorporeal generation is impassionate. But in turn I will ask you, how is he God if a creature? For God is not that which is created—lest I should say that here too in passion—if it should be taken corporeally, as time, conception, thought, hope, pain, danger, failure, correction, all which and more than these are in reference to creation, as is very clear to all. I wonder that you do not dare this, to think of certain individuals united in wedlock, and times of conception and dangers of miscarriage, as if it was not possible for the Father to beget unless he begot in this way. Or

again I wonder, counting up some begotten of birds, creatures of land and sea, that you did not dare to subsume divine and unutterable generation under some one of these, or that you did not dare to take the Son away by your new supposition. You are not able to understand that to the degree to which his generation according to the flesh is different—for where have you known among your own a virgin mother of God?—to this degree even his spiritual generation differs; rather, the degree to which his being is not the same as ours, to this degree even his spiritual generation is removed. The degree to which his being is not the same as ours, to this degree even his generation differs.

(5) Who then is the Father who never began? Someone who has not even begun his being. For whom there is a beginning of being, there is also a beginning of being a father. Therefore he did not later become a Father, for he has no beginning. Rightfully he is Father because he is not also Son. Just as rightfully he is Son because he is not also Father. For these titles are not rightfully ours because we are both. We are not one more than the other. We are from both. Not one, so that we are divided and little by little we become men, and perhaps not men, and such ones as we did not wish, leaving and being left. Thus only the fashions of things remain, bereft of the facts. But an opponent says, "The expression itself 'he begot' and 'he has been begotten'—what other idea do they introduce than a beginning of generation?" Therefore, what if we should say not this but rather "He had been begotten from the beginning," so that we should easily escape your superfluous and time-loving opposition. Then will you bring Scripture against us on the grounds that we are fabricating something against Scripture and the truth? What is this? It is very clear to all that when things are mentioned with reference to time, many things are proposed in reverse order, and especially in the custom of Scripture, not only with the past tense and the present but even in the future. For example, "Why have the nations raged?" [Ps. 2:1]—for not yet had they raged; and, "They will pass through the river on foot" [Ps. 66:6]—which thing they have crossed through. How long it would take to count up all such uses of language, such uses which have been observed by the industrious.

(6) So much on this. But such is their next item, and how very contentious and detestable it is. They state that he begot the Son either voluntarily or involuntarily. Then they suppose that they bind us on both sides with words, yet the cords are not strong but very rotten. For if, as they say, he was involuntarily ruled by some power, who rules over him? And how is he God, if he has been ruled over? But if the Son is voluntarily a son of will, then how is he from the Father? And they fashion a new kind of mother, the will, instead of the Father. Therefore this point is pleasing to them, namely, that in saying this they withdraw from passion and flee for refuge to will. For will is not passion. Second, let us see their strong element in whatever they say. It is best sooner to engage them in a closer struggle. You yourself who speak whatever you would wish, were you brought into existence from your father voluntarily

or involuntarily? If involuntarily, he was ruled over, by force. And who was it who ruled him? You will not say nature, for nature has moderation. But if voluntarily, your father has perished through a few syllables, for you have been shown to be a son of will, not of a father. But I pass over to God and creatures, and I put your question to your wisdom. Did he voluntarily bring all things into existence, or was he forced? If forced, here too is tyranny, and one who ruled by power. But if voluntarily, the creatures were deprived of God, and you before the others, who discover such reasonings and devise such things. Will as a wall is set up in the midst of establisher and creature. But I think that he who wishes and the act of willing are different; so also he who begets and generation, he who speaks and the word—unless we are drunken. On the one hand is he who moves, and on the other, for instance, movement. Therefore that which has been wished is not will, for it does not altogether follow. That which has been begotten is not from generation. That which has been heard is not from pronunciation, but from him who wishes, begot, and spoke. But the things of God transcend all things, with whom perhaps the will of begetting is generation, but there is nothing in the middle (if we should entirely accept this, but not accept that generation is better than will).

(7) Are you willing that I should play some even with "Father"? For it is because of you that I am able to dare such things. God is the Father voluntarily or involuntarily. How will you escape your own dexterity? If voluntarily, when did he begin to wish? It was not before he existed, for there is nothing before him. Or did part of him will and another part was willed? Then he is divided. According to you, as an excuse, how is he not of will? But if involuntarily, what forced him into being? How is he God, if he has been forced, and these things are nothing other than the very being of God? How then was he begotten? How was he created, if, according to you, he was created? This is part of the same difficulty. Perhaps you might say by will and word, but are you not yet saying everything, for how has the will and the word the power of a deed? It still remains to be said. For man was not thus created.

(8) Then how was he begotten? His generation would be nothing great if it was grasped by you who do not know even your own generation or have grasped some little part of it—so little that you are ashamed to speak—then do you suppose that you know all? You would be much weary before you would discover the relations of construction, form, and appearance, and the bond of the soul to the body, mind to soul, reason to mind, movement, growth, assimilation of food, sense, memory, recollection, and the other things from which you have been composed—which are of the soul and body together, which belong to the soul and body independently, which receive from one another. For those whose maturity is later, their relations are from the time of generation. Tell, what are they? Not even then should you inquire into the generation of God. It is not safe. For if you know your own generation, not by any means do you know God's generation. The degree to which God is

harder to trace than man, to a greater degree the heavenly generation is more incomprehensible than your own. But if you say that it has not been grasped by you, and for this reason he has not been begotten, then your hour has come to strike off your list many things which exist, which you have not grasped, and before all things God himself. For you are not able to say whatever he is, even if you are very daring and excessively arrogant. Throw off your flowings and divisions and cuttings, your thinking of incorporeal nature as if corporeal. Then perhaps you would think something worthy of the generation of God. How was he begotten? Again with displeasure I will say this same thing. Let the generation of God be honored by silence. Learning that he was begotten is a great thing for you. But we will not acquiesce that the angels understand how it was, so that we will not acquiesce that you discern it. Do you wish that I should suggest how it was? The Father who begot knows how it was, and the Son who was begotten. Beyond these things, it is hidden by a cloud, escaping your dim sightedness.

(9) Then has he begotten one who exists or one who does not exist? The discussion is nonsense. These are matters about you and me, who on the one hand were existing as something, as Levi in the loins of Abraham [Heb. 7:10], and on the other hand as that which came into existence. Thus in a certain way our condition was that of existing things and nonexisting things. It is contrariwise with material with a beginning which certainly was composed from non-existing things, although some will recast it to be unoriginated. But here "to have been begotten" is even from the beginning in agreement with "to be." So where will you put this dilemma-causing question? For what is older than that which is from the beginning, so that there we should place the previous being of the Son or the nonbeing? In both ways the fact of being from the beginning is destroyed, unless, when we ask again, you would run the risk of saying that the Father is from being and nonbeing, or twofold, partly being before and partly being, or to be in the same case with the Son, that is, to be from nonexisting things. This is because of your sportive questions and your edifices from sand which do not remain firm with breezes [Matt. 7:26-27]. I accept neither of these, and I say that your inquiry is an absurdity, but not difficult to encounter. If it seems necessary to you, according to your dialectic opinions, that one of these choices is always true, then receive from me a little question. Is time in time, or is it not in time? If, therefore, it is in time, in what time? And what is it besides time? And how is it superior? But if it is not in time, what is the uncommon wisdom that introduces timelessness into time? And about the phrase "I now am telling a falsehood," grant one alternative. Either it is true or it is false, for we will not grant both. But it is not possible. For either telling a falsehood he is speaking the truth, or telling the truth he is speaking a falsehood. This must be. Therefore, what is wonderful, as it were, that opposites agree so both are falsehoods, and so to you the wise idea will appear foolish? Still solve for me one riddle. Were you present for your own

generation? And are you now present? Or is neither the case? If you were and are present, as who and with whom? And how have you the one become both? If neither of the things said is the case, how are you separate from yourself? What is the cause of the disjoining? It is boorish to be officious about the one, if he is present to himself or not. For these things are said about others, not oneself. Know well, it is more boorish to settle the question of that begotten from the beginning, if it was before generation or was not. For this is a subject concerning those things divisible in time.

(10) But they state that the unbegotten and the begotten are not the same thing. If this is the case, the Son is not the same as the Father. It is obvious that this reasoning removes the Son or the Father from the deity (why is it necessary to mention it?). If "unbegotten" is the substance of God, "begotten" is not. Yet if the opposite is true, "unbegotten" is not. What reasoning speaks against this? Then, O empty theologian, select whatever impieties you will, if you are completely earnest to act impiously. How then do you say that the unbegotten and the begotten are not the same? If you mean the uncreated and the created are not the same, I accept this, for that which is without beginning and that which *is* created are not the same by nature. But if you mean that which has begotten and that which has been begotten are not the same, the comment is not accurate, for by every necessity they are the same. The nature of the offspring is this: it is the same according to nature to the one who has begotten it. Or again, how do you intend the unbegotten and the begotten? If you mean the very ingenerateness and generation, they are not the same. But if you refer to those who do these things, how are they not the same? Unwisdom and wisdom in and of themselves are not the same; but in relation to man, they are related to the same thing. They do not mark off substance, but they are marked off in relation to the substance itself. Then are immortality, guilelessness, and immutability the substance of God? If this is the case, there are many substances of God, and not one, or the nature of God is composite. He is not these things without composition, if they are substances.

(11) They do not mean these things, for they are also in common with other things. But that which is of God alone and peculiar, this is his substance. Those who bring matter and form together as unbegotten would not acquiesce that the unbegotten is of God alone. (Let us cast further off the darkness of the Manichees). Let it be of God alone. But what about Adam? Is he not alone an image of God? You will say, certainly. Then is he the only man? By no means. Why? Because mankind does not consist of molding. That which has been begotten is man. Thus not only that which is unbegotten is God, although he is the Father alone, but accept that even the begotten is God, for he is of God, even if you are too fond of the term "unbegotten." Then how do you express God's substance not as the thesis of that which is but as the denial of that which is not. The argument discloses that he is not begotten; it does not present what is the nature or condition of that which has no generation. Therefore,

what is the substance of God? You who are officious about generation, it is part of your madness to express this. But for us it will be a great thing if even later we would learn it, when for us the darkness and thickness are destroyed, as the promise of him who does not lie. Let this be thought and hoped for by those who are being purified for this. We will be bold enough to say that if it is a great thing for the Father to be without beginning, it is not less for the Son to be from such a Father, for he would partake of the glory of him who is uncaused, because he is from him who is uncaused, and there is the added fact of generation—a thing so great and thus awesome to those who are not entirely earthbound and material in mentality.

(12) But if they say that according to substance the Son is the same, but that the Father is unbegotten, the Son will also be un-begotten. Well said, if the substance of God is unbegotten so he would be a certain new mixture, begotten-unbegotten. But if the difference is in outside substance, why do you state this as firm? Or are you your father's father, so that in no way you are inferior to your father, since according to substance you are the same? Or is it clear that we will seek the substance of God, whatever it is, if we will seek it, although the specific character remains inviolable. Thus you should learn that unbegotten and God are not the same. If they were the same, it would be absolutely necessary that, since God is God of some one (a relative term) that unbegotten also be of some one (a relative term). Or since unbegotten is of no one (an absolute term), God necessarily must be of some one. The same terms are similarly applied. But unbegotten is not a relative term, for to what is it relative? And of what is God the God? Of all things. Then how would God and unbegotten be the same thing? And again, since the unbegotten and the begotten are contrary to one another as a certain state and privation, it is necessary to conclude that substances have been introduced to one another, being contrary, which very thing has not been given. Or again, since certain states are prior to privations, and privations are destructive of certain states, is it necessary that the Son's substance be prior to the substance of the Father and also be destroyed by the Father, at least on your suppositions?

(13) Still, what inevitable argument remains for them? Perhaps they would flee to this last of all: if God has not stopped begetting, generation is imperfect, and when will he stop? But if he has stopped, he certainly began. Again, carnal individuals have carnal thoughts. But I do not yet say whether he has eternal generation or not, not until I will examine exactly "Before all hills, he begets me" [Prov. 8:25]. But I do not see the necessity of the argument. If according to them that which stopped had begun, then that which will not stop had not begun. Therefore, what will they declare about the soul or the nature of angels? If it had begun, it will also stop. But if it will not stop, it is clear according to them that it had not begun. But it had begun and it will not stop. According to them, that which will stop had not begun. Therefore our argument is as follows: just as in the instance of a horse, ox, or man, of each of them under the

same species, there is one principle. Whatever would partake of the principle, this also properly is to be mentioned. Whatever would not partake, this is not to be mentioned and is not properly to be mentioned. So there is one substance of God, one nature and name, even if names are differentiated by certain determined thoughts. Whatever would be properly said, this is God; and whatever he would be according to nature, this he is truly named, if truth for us is not in names but in facts. But they, having feared lest any stone be unturned against truth, confess that the Son is God, when they are forced by argument and the witnesses of Scripture, but as a namesake sharing only the name.

(14) But when we bring a charge against them: What is this? The Son is not properly God, just as a drawing is not the animal itself? Therefore how is he God, if not properly God? They say, What prevents these things from being ambiguous and both properly stated? And they will mention to us a dog— meaning a beast and a fish, "dog" being ambiguous and stated properly, for there is something and such a species among the ambiguous, and some other thing uses the same name, and shares in it equally, though differing by nature. But here, O dear friend, placing the two natures under the same name, you do not admit that one is better than the other, or that one is prior and the other later, or that the one is more and the other less as regards this which is said. There is no connection which offers this necessity to them. One is not a dog more than the other, and one less, as the "sea" dog than "land" dog, or on the contrary the "land" dog than the "sea" dog. Why should they be, and according to what reason? The commonality of name is among things both of equal honor and differences. But here you yoke an object of worship with God, who is beyond every substance and nature; this is an attribute of God alone and as if the nature of divinity, and you then give this to the Father. But you defraud and subject the Son, assigning to him secondary matters of honor and worship, and even if in written words you freely give equality, in fact you mutilate his divinity and villainously pass over from a verbal identity with equality to one binding unequal things, so that for you a man in writing and a living man proximate divinity, rather than the dogs of the illustration. Or else, grant to both just as a commonality of name so an equal honor of natures, even if you introduced these as differences, and you have destroyed the reference to the dogs which you invented as an example of inequality. What is the advantage of ambiguity and dogs—not that you would prove equality but inequality. How would anyone fighting with himself and divinity be more refuted?

(15) But if, when we say that the Father is greater than the Son in reference to cause, they assume as a premise that he is the cause by nature and then they infer that he is the greater by nature, then I do not know whether they are by false reasoning cheating themselves or the ones against whom there is the argument. For not absolutely can all things predicated of a class be also predicated of each that composes it, but it is clear different particulars that

belong to different ones. What hinders me is this proposition that the Father is greater by nature—then the addition—but not entirely by nature greater nor father—with its inference from this that the greater is not entirely greater nor the Father entirely Father. But if you wish it in this way: God is substance, but the substance is not altogether God. You yourself infer from what follows: God is not altogether God. But, I think, this is the fallacy in an argument from the conditioned to the absolute, as in the custom for those who speak technically about these things. For when we grant "greater" to the nature of his cause, they apply "the greater" to the nature. Just as if we would say that such a one was a dead man, they themselves simply apply it to mean that he was a man.

(16) But how should we rush past the following, which is not less admirable than the things said? They say that the Father is a name of substance or action, so binding us on both sides. If we say a name of substance they will agree that the Son is of another substance since the substance of God is one, and this, as they say, the Father has taken possession of previously. But if we say a name of action, clearly we will confess that the Son is a work but not an offspring. For where there is the worker, there is that which is worked upon. And they will say that they wonder how the thing which is made is the same as he who made it. Even I myself would exceedingly fear your division if it was necessary to accept one or the other of the two and not rather to escape the two to state a third more true, that the Father is a name neither of a substance, O most clever ones, nor of an action, but that the Father is the name of the relation in which the Father is to the Son or the Son to the Father. For, as among us, the titles themselves make known a genuine and suitable thing. Even here they indicate the identity of nature of the one begotten to that which begot. But let it be your pleasure: the Father is a certain substance. This will bring in with it the Son; it will not estrange him according to common thoughts and the power of these names. And let it be a name of action, if this seems good. You will not thus convict us. This result itself of action would be the *homoousion*, for if otherwise the understanding of action in this case would be absurd. You see how we escape your perversions, although you wish to fight wickedly. But since we have known your invincibility in arguments and perversions, let us look at your strength from divine sayings if then you would take from them to persuade us.

(17) From their great and exalted discourses we have discovered and preached the deity of the Son. What discourses are these? Namely, God, the Word, who was in the beginning, with the beginning, the beginning. "In the beginning was the Word and the Word was with God and the Word was God" [John 1:1] and "With you is the beginning" [Ps. 110:3] and "He who calls her a beginning from generations" [Isa. 41:4]. Then there is the only-begotten Son, "the only-begotten Son, who is in the bosom of the Father, that one has declared him" [John 1:18]. A way, truth, life, light: "I am the way, the truth, and the life" [John 14:6] and "I am the light of the world" [John 8:12]. Wisdom, power:

"Christ, the power of God and the wisdom of God" [1 Cor. 1:24]. Reflection, impress, image, seal: "He who is a reflection of the glory and the impress of his *hypostasis*" [Heb. 1:3] and "image of goodness" [Wisd. of Sol. 7:26] and "God the Father sealed him" [John 6:27]. Lord, King, he who is, the all-sovereign: "The Lord rained fire from the Lord" [Gen. 19:24] and "The scepter of your kingdom is a scepter of justice" [Ps. 45:6] and "He who is, who was, and the one who comes, and the all-sovereign" [Rev. 1:8]. These statements are clearly about the Son, as there are many of identical power as these, none of which is an addition or added later to the Son or the Spirit or to the Father himself. For perfection is not from addition. There was not when he was Wordless, or when he was not the Father. Nor was there when he was not true, not wisdom, not powerful, not lacking life or splendor or goodness.

(18) But against these you count for me phrases indicating ignorance. "My God and your God" [John 20:17], "greater" [John 14:28], "he created" [Prov. 8:22], "he made" [Acts 2:36], "he sanctified" [John 10:36]. And, if you wish, "slave" [Phil. 2:7], "obedient" [Phil. 2:8], "he gave" [John 18:11], "he learned" [Heb. 5:8], "he was ordered" [John 5:36], "he is not able of himself to do anything" [John 8:28], or to say "to judge" [John 8:15], "to give" [Matt. 20:23], "to wish" [John 5:20]. And also there are these: ignorance [Mark 13:32], subjection [Luke 2:51], prayer [Luke 3:21], request [Luke 22:41], advance [Luke 2:40], becoming perfect [Heb. 2:10]. If you wish, add many more lowly than these: sleep [Matt. 8:24], hunger [Matt. 21:28], exhaustion [John 4:6], weeping [John 11:35], striving, submitting [Luke 22:44]. Perhaps you would reproach his cross and death. For you think it best to leave to me the resurrection and ascension, since among these something is found that befits our side. And even in addition to these you could babble about many things, if you would wish to put together your ambiguous and interpolated god, but a God who is for us true and equal in honor. It is not difficult to go through in turn each of these and to interpret to you most piously and to clear away the cause of stumbling in the texts—that is, if you are actually stumbling and not willingly doing evil. In short, apply the higher things to the Godhead, to the nature better than sufferings and the body. But apply the more humble things to the compounded one, who has been emptied for your sake and has become incarnate. It is nothing worse to say "And he became man and then has been exalted" in order that you, when you have dismissed your sensual and fruitless teaching, would learn to be more lofty and to rise with the Godhead. You would not be content among visible things, but you would rise together with things of thought, and you would know what is the law of his nature and what is the law of his economy.

(19) This one who now is disdained by you was once and was above you. He who is now a human being was also uncompounded. That which he was, he continued; but that which he was not, he assumed. In the beginning he was without cause, for who is the cause of God? But later because of a cause

he came into existence, associated with flesh through the means of the mind, and became a human being, the God below. (This cause was the salvation of insolent you, you who on this account despised his deity so that he received your materiality. Thus he was mixed with God and became one, the better conquered, so that I might become God as he became man. He was begotten and born, from a woman but a virgin. There were two elements: one human, one divine. Humanly he was fatherless, divinely he was motherless. But the whole is of the deity. He was in the womb, but he was known by the prophet, even himself being in the womb, leaping before the Word, on account of whom he came into being [Luke 1:41]. He was wrapped in swaddling clothes, but he tore off the clothes of the grave when he arose [Luke 24:12]. He was placed in a manger, but he was glorified by angels [Luke 2:9] and disclosed by a star and worshiped by wise men. Why do you stumble over that which is seen, not looking at that which is thought? He was banished into Egypt, but he banished the idols of the Egyptians. He did not have form or beauty among the Jews, but to David he was, in the prime of life, more beautiful than the sons of men [Isa. 53:2]; but on the mountain he flashed forth, and he became more radiant than the sun, leading us into the mysteries of the future [Matt. 17:2].

(20) He was baptized as a human being, but he remitted sins as God; he did not require purifications himself but that he might sanctify the waters. He was tempted as a human being, but he conquered as God; he exhorts us to be of good cheer, because he has conquered the world [John 16:33]. He hungered, but he nourished thousands; he is heaven's bread of life. He thirsted, but he shouted, "If anyone thirsts, let him come to me and let him drink" [John 6:35]. He also offered springs of water to believers. He was tired, but he is a rest for the weary and heavy-laden [Matt. 11:28]. He was overcome with sleep, but he was lifted on the sea; he rebuked the winds, and he lifted up Peter, who was being submerged [Matt. 14:24, 31]. He pays taxes, but from a fish; he is king of those who demand them [Matt. 17:27]. As a Samaritan and a demoniac, he listens, but he saves the one who came down from Jerusalem and fell among thieves (John 8:48; Luke 10:30-37]; he is recognized by demons and drives them away; he immerses a legion of spirits and sees the prince of demons falling as lightning [Mark 5:9]. He is stoned, but he is not conquered [John 8:59]. He prays, but he listens. He weeps, but he stops tears. He asks where Lazarus is, for he was a human being; but he raises Lazarus, for he was God [John 11:34, 35, 43]. He is sold, and at a very low price—thirty pieces of silver—but he redeems the world, and at a great cost: his own blood. As a sheep he is led to the slaughter, but he is shepherd of Israel and now the entire world [Isa. 53:7; Ps. 80:1]. As a lamb, he is speechless, but he is the Word, announced by the voice of him who cries in the wilderness. He bears infirmity and is wounded, but he heals every disease and every weakness [Matt. 9:35]. He is lifted up to the tree, he is affixed to the cross, but he will restore us by the tree of life [Rev. 22:2; Gen. 2:9]. He saves even the robber being crucified; he

made dark every visible thing. He is given sour wine to drink; he is fed gall. Who is this? He who has turned water into wine, the destroyer of bitter taste, sweetness and every desire [Song of Sol. 5:16]. He hands over his soul, but he has the power to receive it again; the veil is torn, for the heavenly things are exhibited; the rocks are split; the dead rise [Matt. 27:51-52]. He dies, but he makes alive, and by his death he destroys death. He is buried, but he arises. He goes down into hell, but he leads up the souls. He goes up into heaven, and he will come to judge the living and dead, to test such words as yours. But these things create for you the pretext of error; those things demolish your error.

(21) These things are for the sake of those who are fond of riddles among us. We did not willingly reply, for frivolity and the opposition of arguments are not sweet for the faithful. One adversary is enough, but we replied of necessity, because of those who break in (since medicines are for the sake of the ill), so that they would see that they are not all-knowing nor unconquerable in superfluous things that make the Gospel void. When we, leaving the faith, would put forth the power of argument and destroy the credibility of the Spirit by inquiries, then the argument becomes weaker than the greatness of the topics—and it will always be weaker, because it is motivated by the weak instrument of our mind—what happens? The weakness of the argument appears to be part of the mystery, and thus the cleverness of the argument declares the nullification of the cross, as Paul also teaches [1 Cor. 1:17]. For faith is the completion of our argument, but he who announces bonds of the universe and looses the things held fast, he who put it in our minds to break apart the knots of forced beliefs, may he, especially after he changed these individuals, make them to be faithful instead of logic-choppers, and Christians instead of that which they are now named. We then exhort this, we beg, on behalf of Christ. Become reconciled to God and do not quell the Spirit [2 Cor. 5:20]. Rather, may Christ be reconciled to you, and may the Spirit inflame you, although it is late. But if you are very fond of strife, may we preserve for our very selves the Trinity and be saved by the Trinity, remaining uncorrupted and void of offense until the more perfect display of those things which are desired, in him Christ our Lord, to whom be glory into the ages. Amen.

12

Gregory of Nyssa's Concerning We Should Think of Saying That There Are Not Three Gods to Ablabius

It is right that you, who are in the prime of every interior resource, contend against the enemies of truth and do not shrink from your toils, so that we as fathers might be cheered by the noble labor of our children. The law of nature lays down this very thing as a principle. But since you have turned the battle array and released against us the assaults of barbs, which those opposed to truth throw, and you exhort that with the shield of faith the solitary hot coals be extinguished by us old men (Ps. 120:4) and the sharpened arrows of so-called knowledge be removed, we accept the injunction. Thus we become for you a model of ready obedience, so that you would yourself supply to us in turn an equal payment for like injunctions if at some time we might call you to such conflicts, O Ablabius, noble soldier of Christ.

This is not a minor subject which you have put forward for us, nor is it such a kind to cause slight damage, if it were not met with a befitting review. The force of the inquiry necessarily brings one into one of two altogether incompatible positions. One is according to common opinion: to say that there are three gods, which is wicked. The other: not to bear witness to the deity of the Son and the Spirit, which is ungodly and absurd. Your statement is of such a kind: Peter, James, and John, being in one humanity, are called three men. And it is not absurd that those united according to nature, if they are several, be counted in the plural on the basis of the term "nature." If therefore usage here permits this, and no one forbids the statement of two as two or of three as beyond two, how, in reference to the mystical beliefs in the confession that there are three *hypostases*, and the claim that there is no difference between them in nature, do we struggle somehow with the confession by declaring there is one deity of Father, Son, and Spirit but by forbidding the statement that there are three gods?

As I said before, the topic has much that is hard to manage. But if we might find something by which the ambiguity of our mind will be supported, so that in this strange dilemma it no longer doubts and grieves, it would be well. But if our reasoning would be proven unequal to the task, we will guard the tradition we received from the fathers as always firm and immovable. We will seek from the Lord the word of faith as an advocate. If this would be found by anyone of those who have the grace, we will give thanks to him who gave the grace. If not, nevertheless, on the basis of what is known we will keep the unchangeable faith.

Why then in our usage, when we reckon those who are shown to be one in nature, do we name them in the plural? We say that the men are so many and that not all are "one," but in reference to the divine nature the argument of doctrine rejects the multitude of gods and counting the *hypostases* does not admit a plural meaning.

If someone were speaking superficially to simpler minds, he would seem to say that the argument in fleeing the likeness of Greek polytheism shuns counting the gods by number, so that no one would think there is a commonality of doctrine between the Greeks and us, if like them, we counted the divinity not in the singular but in the plural. This statement to the more simple would perhaps appear to be something. But with reference to those who seek that for themselves, one of the two propositions should stand—either not to confess the deity of the three, or to name the three together as those who share the same deity—and such a reply does not resolve the question. Therefore it is necessary that the answer be made more fully and that as much as possible we trace the truth. The topic is not about ordinary things.

First, we acknowledge that there is an abuse of usage when those who are not determined by nature, according to the term itself, are named in the plural, and when it is said that there are many men. It is similar to saying that there are many human natures. That such is the case is clear to us from what follows. When summoning someone, we do not address him by his nature, for the common character of the name would produce a certain error, since each hearer thinks he himself is the one summoned because the calling is not by the peculiar name but by the common name of the nature. But we separate him from the many by saying the word peculiarly imposed on him (I mean the signification of the subject), for there are many who shared the nature— for example, disciples, apostles, martyrs—but one is the "man" in all, if as has been said "man" does not mean the peculiarity of each but the common nature. For Luke or Stephan is a man. But if anyone is a man, is he not by any means Luke or Stephan.

But through the perceived peculiarities, the topic of the individual *(hypostases)* admits distinction and is viewed in number according to combination. But the nature is one; it is united to itself, undivided, a precisely undivided unit, not increased through addition, not decreased through subtraction, but being one and remaining one, even if it would appear in a multitude, undivided, continuous, perfect, and not divided by those who individually share it. And just as a people, a common folk, an army, and an assembly is always mentioned as singular but each is discovered in the plural, so in accord with the most precise reasoning also "man" properly should be said as one (singular), even if those shown to be in the same nature would be plural. Thus it would be much better to improve our blundered usage and no longer extend the name for nature to the plural than for us enslaved to carry over the identical error even to divine doctrine. But since the improvement of usage is impractical (How would anyone be persuaded not to say many men when they are shown to be of the same nature? Usage is always unchangeable) in reference to the lower nature, in not opposing the current usage, we would not be far wrong. There is no loss here from the wrong employment of words. But in reference to divine doctrine, the indifferent employment of words is no longer, similarly, without danger, for here "minor" points are not minor.

Therefore one God must be confessed by us according to the witness of Scripture, "Hear, Israel, the Lord your God is one Lord" (Deut. 6:4), even if the word "deity" extends through the holy Trinity. But I say these things according to the reasoning given by us in reference to human nature, by which we have learned that it is necessary to extend the word for nature to the plural. But the word for deity must be scrutinized more accurately by us, so that through the significance inherent in the term there might be some assistance in regard to the truth of the subject under discussion.

Therefore the word for deity seems to many peculiarly to be fixed on God's nature. As the heaven, the sun, or some other of the elements of the world is explained by peculiar names which signify the subjects, so they say in reference to the highest and divine nature that the word for deity has been suitably adapted, as some proper name, to that which is made clear. But we, following the suggestions of Scripture, have learned that the divine nature is unnameable and unutterable. We say that every name, whether it has been invented from human usage or handed down from Scripture, is an interpretation of the things thought about divine nature and does not encompass the significance of the nature itself.

This state of affairs could be shown without much diligent study. Anyone would find that the remaining names—as many as refer to creation, and quite apart from any deviation—by chance are well-fitted to the subjects. However, we are content that things are noted by their names, so that we escape confession in our knowledge of those things. But as many names as there are for guidance to divine knowledge, each contains its peculiar meaning, and you would not find any term among the names more fitting to God without some meaning. Thus it is shown from this that the divine nature itself is not noted by any of the names, but that something of its characteristics is made known through the statements. For we state, perchance, that the divine is incorruptible, or powerful, or as many other things as it is customary to say. But we find in each of the names a peculiar reflection suitable to be thought and said about the divine nature, but not signifying what that nature is according to its substance. Whatever this is, it is incorruptible, but the idea of the incorruptible is this: that which it is, is not to be reconciled with corruptibility. Therefore, in saying that it is incorruptible, we say that his nature is that which does not suffer. But we have not suggested what it is that does not suffer corruption. Thus if we would say it is that which makes alive, although we have signified what it does by its name, we have not made known by the word the thing which does it. And according to the same reasoning, we find in all the other instances that the significance connected with divine names is either in their forbidding the incorrect knowledge in reference to the divine nature or in their teaching that which is correct. But we do not find them encompassing an explanation of the nature itself.

Therefore, then, observing the various activities of the transcendent power from each of the activities known to us, we fit together the names. This one is activity-energy, viewing and seeing a vision we speak of God, and as someone might say, beholding. Accordingly he sees all things and oversees all, as he sees the thoughts when he passes through even invisible things by his power of viewing. Thus we have assumed that "deity" has been named from "view" (*theotes* from *thea*) and our observer is named God from custom and the teaching of Scripture.

But if someone agrees that to view and to see is the same thing, and that the God who oversees all both is and is called overseer of all, let him calculate God's energy activity, whether it is present in one of the persons believed to be in the holy Trinity or whether the power pervades through the three.

If the interpretation of deity is true, and visible things are beheld, and that which beholds is called God, then not reasonably would any of the persons in the Trinity be separated from such a name because of the significance of the name. Scripture bears witness to the seeing equally of the Father, Son, and Holy Spirit. "See, God, our protector," says David [Ps. 84:9]. From this we learn that, as far as God is thought out, the activity of sight is appropriate to God. David said, "See, God." But also Jesus sees the thoughts of those who pass sentence on him, since by his supreme authority he remits men's sins. For it states, "Jesus, having seen their thoughts" [Matt. 9:4]. And concerning the Spirit, Peter says to Ananias, "Why has Satan filled your heart so you are false to the Holy Spirit?" [Acts 5:3]. This reveals that the Holy Spirit was a truthful and knowledgeable witness of the things dared in secret by Ananias. It was through the Spirit that these things done in secret were disclosed to Peter. For Ananias himself, as he thought, escaping the notice of all and concealing his sin, became a thief of his own goods. But the Holy Spirit was with Peter and observed the covetous intent of Ananias, and through himself the Spirit gave to Peter the ability to discern these secrets. It is clear that the Spirit could not do this if he were blind to secret things.

But someone will say that the proof of the argument does not apply to the topic under investigation. For if it would be acknowledged that the name for deity applies to nature, this does not already prove that it is improper to speak of gods. Quite the opposite, we are compelled to speak of gods. For in reference to human usage, we find not only the many as the sharers of the same nature, but even certain individuals of the same pursuit are mentioned not individually. Accordingly, as we say, many orators, land-measurers, husbandmen, shoemakers, etc. And if the reference point for the term "deity" were nature, it would have the occasion, in accord with the previous argument, to comprehend the three persons individually and to speak of one God, because of the indivisible and inseparable character of the nature. But since it has been proven by means of the things said that the name of deity signifies activity and not nature, the argument as a result of the things proven turns in the opposite direction. Thus it is necessary rather to speak of three gods who are viewed in the same activity, as they say that three philosophers or orators are mentioned, or if there is any other name from a pursuit when there are many who share the same thing. I have more industriously worked at these things, namely, the argument of the opposing objections, so that our doctrine would be more firmly fixed, strengthened by the persistences of the contradictions. Therefore the argument again must be resumed.

Since it has been shown by us with reason and by proof that the name of deity has not as its reference point nature but activity, perhaps someone would declare with reason why men who share with one another the same pursuits are counted and named in the plural but the deity is mentioned in the singular as one God and one deity, even if the three *hypostases* are not distinguished from the significance reflected in "deity." He might state that as regards men, even if many partake of one activity, each individually set apart work at the thing proposed, sharing in common nothing with the individual activity of those pursuing the same thing. For if the orators are many, among the several the pursuit has one and the same name, but those who pursue it work each individually, this one practicing oratory independently, the next one doing the same thing. Therefore, among men, because the activity of each is distinguished, although in the same pursuit, they are properly mentioned in the plural. Each of them is separated into his peculiar context from the others in accord with his peculiar manner of the activity. But in reference to divine nature, we have learned that this is not the case, because the Father does something individually, in which the Son does not join, or the Son individually works something without the Spirit; but every activity which pervades from God to creation and is named according to our manifold designs starts off from the Father, proceeds through the Son, and is completed by the Holy Spirit. On account of this, the name of activity is not divided into the multitude of those who are active. The action of each in any regard is not divided and peculiar. But whatever of the anticipated things would happen, whether for our providence or to the administration of the whole and to its constitution, it happens through the three, the things which do happen are not three distinct things.

We will think through this statement from one certain example, from him, I mean, the crown of free gifts. As many things as have a share in this gift gain life. Therefore, when we ask from where this good thing came to us, we find through the guidance of the Scriptures that it is from the Father, Son, and Holy Spirit. But though we presuppose that there are three persons and names, we do not reason that three lives have been given to us—individually one from each of them. It is the same life, activated by the Holy Spirit, prepared by the Son, and produced by the Father's will.

Therefore, then, the holy Trinity works every activity according to the manner stated, not divided according to the number of the *hypostases*, but one certain motion and disposition of goodwill occurs, proceeding from the Father through the Son to the Spirit. Thus we do not say that those who effect one life are three who make alive, nor do we say that they are three good beings who are viewed in the same goodness, nor as regards all other aspects do we announce them in the plural. Thus we are not able to name as three those who bring to bear on us and all creation jointly and inseparably this divine power and activity of oversight. When we learned about the God of all, as Scripture says that he judges the whole earth [Gen. 8:25; Rom. 8:6], thus we say that he is the judge of all. And when we heard that the Father judges no one [John 5:22], we do not think that Scripture wars with itself. For he who judges all the earth does it through the Son, to whom he has given all judgment. And everything that happens by the Only-begotten has reference to the Father, so he is judge of all and through the whole judges no one. As it was stated, he has given judgment to the Son, and all the judgment of the Son is not estranged from the Father's will. It cannot with reason be said either that there are two judges, or that one is estranged from authority and power of judgment. Thus also in reference to the word for deity, Christ is the power of God and the wisdom of God. The power of oversight and beholding—which we say is deity, the Father, the God doing all things in wisdom—effects through the Only-begotten, the Son who perfects all power in the Holy Spirit and judges. As Isaiah says, "by the spirit of judgment and the spirit of burning heat" [Isa. 4:4]. Therefore, according to the discourse of the Gospel, which he made to the Jews, he does well by the Spirit of God, for he says, "If I by the Spirit of God cast out demons" [Matt. 12:28]; from his sharing in doing well, he comprehends every form through the unity of activity. The term for activity is not able to be distributed into many, by whom through one another a single thing is effected.

For, as it has been stated above, the principle of the power of oversight and beholding in Father, Son, and Holy Spirit is one. It starts off from the Father as from a spring; it is effected by the Son, and by the power of the Spirit it completes its grace. No activity is divided to the *hypostases*, completed individually by each and set apart without being viewed together. All providence, care, and attention of all, both of things in the sensible creation and of things of the heavenly nature—and the preservation of what exists, the correction of things out of tune, the teaching of things set right —is one and not three, kept straight by the holy Trinity. It is not severed into three, according to the number of persons beheld in faith, so that each activity, viewed by itself, is of the Father alone or of the Only-begotten individually or of the Holy Spirit separately. As the apostle says, "The one and the same Spirit distributes to each privately the good things" [1 Cor. 12:11], The movement of good from the Spirit is not without beginning. We find that the power thought of as proceeding it, which is the only-begotten God, does all things, without whom nothing of the things which exist comes into origin. Again this spring of good things started from the Father's will.

If every good thing, and the name for it, is attached to a power and will without beginning, it is brought into perfection at once and apart from time by the power of the Spirit through the only-begotten God. No postponement occurs, or is thought of, in the movement of divine will from the Father through the Son to the Spirit. But deity is one of the good names and thoughts, and not reasonably is the name to be used in the plural, since the unity of activity prevents a plural counting.

And the Father, Savior of all men, especially of the faithful, has been named by the apostle as one [1 Tim. 4:10]. No one on the basis of this term says that the Son does not save those who believe, or that salvation happens to those who share it apart from the Spirit. But God, who is over all, becomes the Savior of all, while the Son effects salvation by the grace of the Spirit. On account of this they are not named three saviors by Scripture, although salvation is confessed from the holy Trinity. Thus, according to the significance of deity already granted, there are not three gods, even if such a name coincides with the holy Trinity.

It does not seem to me to be particularly necessary as a present proof of the argument to fight against those who gainsay that it is not necessary to think of the "deity" as activity. We believe that the divine nature is indeterminate and uncircumscribed, so we do not think of its comprehension, but we define that the nature be thought of in every way as infinity. The infinite usually is not defined by anything or by anyone, but according to every argument infinity escapes limits. Therefore that which is beyond limit is not at all defined by a name. Thus, in reference to the divine nature, in order that the intent of the indeterminate might remain, we say that the divine is above every name, and one of the names is deity. Therefore the same thing is not able to be a name and to be thought to be above every name.

If again the idea that the significance is not in reference to activity but nature seems attractive to our adversaries, we turn back the argument to the beginning, namely, the custom mistakenly refers a plural significance to a term for nature. According to true reason, neither reduction nor growth occurs to nature when it is viewed in larger or small things. According to usage, only those who are numbered that are viewed according to a peculiar circumscription. This circumscription *is* comprehended by appearance of a body, size, location, and difference in shape and color. But that which transcends these things that are viewed escapes the circumscription of such things. That which is not circumscribed is not numbered; that which is not numbered is not able to be viewed in size.

When we speak of gold, even if it is changed into many stamps of a coin, still it is, and is mentioned as, one. But we name many current coins and many staters [a small coin], although we find no increase of the nature of gold by reason of the number of the staters. Therefore much gold is mentioned when it is viewed in larger weight either in vessels or in coins. But "many golds" are not named because of the quantity of the material, unless someone would say "many golds," as darks or staters, in reference to which it is not the material but the small coins that receive the significance of the number. It is properly said not that there are "many golds" but that there are "many golden ones."

Therefore just as the golden staters are many but gold is one, thus those who are individually in the nature of man are revealed as many, for example, Peter, James, and John. But the "man" in them is one. Even if Scripture extends the name to a plural significance in the statements "Men swear by the greater" [Heb. 6:16] and "sons of men," etc., one must know that it uses the custom of prevailing language. It does not make laws about what way it is proper to use words, nor in doing these things does it give technical teaching about words. It uses the word according to the prevailing custom, looking only to this, that the word might become useful to those who receive it. It is not precise in language in relation to speech, where no damage concerning the intention of words involved.

A count of the incorrect combinations of the word in Scripture to prove what has been said would be long. But where there is a danger that something of the truth could be damaged, no longer does one find in the written words an unquestioning and indifferent state of affairs. Therefore it accedes to the plural usage of "men," because no one by supposition would fall by such a form of the word into a quantity of "humanities" or think that many human natures are signified through the plural use of the name for nature. But by close observation it uses the word "God" according to a singular pattern, providing for this, so that different natures of the divine substance are not introduced secretly by the plural significance of "gods." Therefore it says, "The Lord God is one Lord" [Deut. 6:4], but it also proclaims by the word for deity the only-begotten of God, and it does not break up the one into a dual significance, so to name the Father and Son as two gods, even if each is proclaimed God by the holy authors. The Father is God, the Son is God, but by the same proclamation

God is one, because neither in regard to nature nor activity is any difference viewed.

If, according to the supposition of those who are mistaken, the nature in the holy Trinity has been varied, then it results that the number would extend to a quantity of gods, divided by the difference of their subjects' substance. But since the divine single and unchangeable nature rejects every difference in substance so that it would be one, it does not allow by itself a plural significance. Just as the nature is said to be one, all the other aspects are named individually in the singular, God, good, holy, savior, righteous judge, and whatever other of the names befitting God comes to mind, which someone, looking either to his nature or activity, mentions. On this point we will not differ. But if anyone would slander this argument as by not admitting the difference in nature, it prepares some mixture and interchange of the *hypostases*; concerning such a reproach we will defend the argument. While confessing the un-changeableness of the nature, we do not deny the difference in cause and causality, by which alone we seize the distinction of the one from the other. It is by the belief that one is the cause and the other is from the cause. We also consider another difference of the one who is from the cause. There is the one which depends on the first, and there is that one which is through that which depends on the first. Thus it is that the aspect of only-begotten undoubtedly remains in the Son. It is also not doubted that the Spirit is from the Father. The mediation of the Son, although it guards for him his only-begottenness, does not prevent the Spirit from a relation by nature to the Father.

But speaking of a "cause" and "from a cause," we do not through these names signify "nature" (for no one would grant that the word for cause and nature is the same), but we disclose the difference in the manner of being. Saying that one thing is caused but another is without cause, we did not separate the nature by reason of the cause. We have only disclosed that the Son does not exist unbegotten, nor the Father through begetting. First it is necessary for us to believe that something is, and then to be inquisitive about how that which is believed is, for example, its manner of existence. Therefore the topic of what is, is one thing. It is another manner how it is (its manner of existence). Thus, to say something exists unbegotten suggests how it is, but what it is, is not disclosed by this word. If you questioned a farmer about some tree, whether it is planted or exists by chance, and he answered either that the tree is not planted or that it happened from a planting, then through the answer does he who only said how it is disclose the nature, or does he leave the principle of the nature unknown and uninterpreted?

Thus also here, having learned that he is unbegotten, we have been taught how it is fitting to think of his being, but we do not hear from the word whatever it is. Therefore in saying that there is such a difference in the holy Trinity so to believe that one is the cause and another from the cause, we would no longer be accused with dissolving the principle of the *hypostases* in a commonality of nature. Then the principle of cause distinguishes the *hypostases* in the holy Trinity in worshiping that which is uncaused and the other which is from the cause. But the divine nature is comprehended by every thought as unchangeable and without difference. On account of this, there is properly one deity and one God, and all other aspects of names befitting God are reported in the singular.

13

Augustine of Hippo's On the Trinity, Book 9

(1) Indeed, we seek a trinity, yet not any one, but that trinity which is God, the true, greatest, and only God. Therefore, whoever hears these things, be patient, for we are seeking to this point. No one justly reproves the individual who seeks such things, if as a person most steadfast he seeks that which is most difficult either to know or to declare. Whoever sees and teaches better, quickly and justly reproves him who makes assertions. He says, "Seek the Lord and your soul will live" [Ps. 69:32]. And lest anyone delight as if he had by chance laid hold of him, he says, "Seek always his face" [Ps. 105:4]. And the apostle says, "If anyone thinks that he knows anything, he does not yet know how it is proper for him to know. However, whoever loves God, he has been known by him" [1 Cor. 8:2-3]. Thus he said not that he "knew him," which is a perilous presumption, but that he "has been known by him." Thus, elsewhere when he had said, "now knowing God . . . ," correcting himself at once, he said, rather, "having been known by God . . . " [Gal. 4:9]. And especially in that passage he said, "Brothers, I do not think that I myself laid hold; however, one thing I do, forgetting which things are in the past. Having hastened, I follow purposely into the things that are before, toward the palm of victory of God's high calling in Christ Jesus. Therefore, let us, however many, discern this" [Phil. 3:13-15]. He says that perfection in this life is nothing other than to forget "these things which are in the past" and "purposely to hasten to these things which are before." The safest intention for him who seeks is to seek until that for which we strive and we hasten is laid hold of. Thus the correct intention originates from faith. In some way a certain faith begins knowledge, but a certain knowledge will not be accomplished unless it is after this life, when we will see "face to face" [1 Cor. 13:12]. Let us discern this, so that we know that seeking truth is safer than presuming unknown things for known. Let us seek as if we were about to find, and let us find as if we were about to seek. "When a man has finished, then he begins" [Ecclus. 18:6].

Let us not doubt with unfaithfulness about things to be believed; let us assert without rashness about things to be understood. In the former, authority must be seized; in the latter, truth sought. Therefore, with respect to this issue, let us believe that the Father and Son and Holy Spirit are one God, creator and ruler of the entire creature, and that the Father is not the Son, nor the Holy Spirit the Father or the Son, but that there is a trinity of mutually related persons and a unity of equal substance. Let us seek to understand this from that very one, whom invoking, we wish to understand; and to the degree that it is given to us to understand, let us seek to expound with so much care and solicitude of piety that even if we say something for something else, we should say nothing unworthy. So if, for example, we say anything concerning the Father which does not peculiarly befit the Father, it may befit the Son or the Holy Spirit or the Trinity itself. And if we say something concerning the Son which does not peculiarly suit the Son, at least it may suit the Father or the Holy Spirit or the Trinity. Likewise, if we say anything concerning the Holy Spirit which does not teach a property of the Holy Spirit, may it not, however, be alien to the Father or to the Son or to the one God, the Trinity itself. Now we desire to see whether that most excellent love *(caritas)* is peculiar to the Holy Spirit. If it is not, then the Father is love, or the Son, or the Trinity itself, since we are not able to oppose the most certain faith and most influential authority of Scripture saying, "God is love" [1 John 4:16]. We ought not turn aside in a sacrilegious error so that we say something about the Trinity which befits not the creator but rather the creature, or is devised by empty thinking.

(2) Since such is the case, let us direct our attention to these three items which we have apparently discovered. We are speaking not yet about celestial matters, not yet about God the Father, the Son, and the Holy Spirit, but about this inferior image but yet an image, that is, man. The weakness of our mind may more familiarly and easily contemplate this.

Behold, when I who seek this love something, this involves three things: I, that which I love, and love itself. I do not love a person who loves, for there is not love where nothing is loved. Therefore there are three: a person who loves, that which is loved, and love. What if I love only myself? Will there be two— love and what I love? For the person loving and that which is loved, this is the same when he loves himself, just as to love and to be loved in the same way are the very same when someone loves himself. Obviously, the same thing is said twice when it is said, "He loves himself and he is loved by himself." Then to love and to be loved are not different things, just as the person loving and loved is different. But, in truth, love and that which is loved—even these are two—for there is not love when someone loves himself, except when love itself is loved. It is different to love oneself and to love one's own love. For love is not loved except now already loving something, because where nothing is loved, there is no love. Therefore there are two when someone loves himself—love and that which is loved—for then the person loving and that which is loved are one. From this it does not seem to be reasonable that where love is, three things should be understood.

Let us exclude from consideration the fact that there are many elements from which man is composed, and that these things, which now we seek, we may clearly discover, as far as we are able. Let us examine the mind alone. The mind when it loves itself reveals two certain things: the mind and love. But what is to love oneself except to wish to be present with oneself for the enjoyment of self? And when he wishes himself to be so much as he is, will is equal to mind, and love is equal to him who loves. And if love is some substance, it certainly is not a body but spirit. And the mind is not a body but spirit. However, love and mind are not two spirits but one spirit, not two substances but one. However, the two are one, the person who loves and love— or, you would say, that which is loved and love. These two are certainly said to be mutually related. Indeed, the person loving is referred to love, and love to the person loving. The person who loves, loves with some love, and love is a characteristic of someone loving. Indeed, mind and spirit are not mentioned relatively but describe substance, for there are mind and spirit not because they are a characteristic of some man. After the body has been withdrawn from this which is man, that which he is called after the body has been added, the mind and spirit remain. However, after the person who loves has been withdrawn, there is no love, and after love has been withdrawn, there is no person loving. Thus, as far as they are mutually related they are two, but they are also mentioned in respect to themselves, and each is spirit, and both at the same time are one spirit; and each is mind and at the same time one mind. Therefore, where is the Trinity? As far as we are able, let us direct our attention and let us invoke the eternal light, so that it lightens our darkness and so that, as far as we are allowed, we may see the image of God in ourselves.

(3) The mind is not able to love itself unless it also knows itself. For how docs it love what it does not know? If anyone says that the mind believes itself to be such by a general or special knowledge, of such a kind as it has experienced at another time, and therefore to love itself, this person is speaking most foolishly. Where does a mind know another mind if it does not know itself? For not as an eye of the body sees other eyes and does not see itself, so does the mind know other minds and is ignorant of its very self. Through the eyes of the body we see bodies, because we are unable to break up and bend back into themselves the rays that shine through them and touch whatever we see distinctly, except when we look at mirrors. The topic is discussed most exactly and obscurely until it is shown most clearly whether the matter is thus or not. But whatever the character of the face by which we see distinctly through the eyes, we are certainly not capable of seeing the face itself with the eyes, whether they are rays or some other thing, but we seek in the mind and, if it is possible, we also apprehend this with the mind. Therefore the mind itself, as it gathers knowledge of corporeal things through the senses of the body, gathers through itself knowledge of incorporeal things. Therefore, because it

is incorporeal it knows itself through itself. If it does not know itself, it does not love itself.

(4) Thus there are two specific things: the mind and its love, when it loves itself. So there are two specific things: the mind and its knowledge, when it knows itself. Therefore the mind itself, love, and its knowledge are three specific things, and these three are one, and when they are perfect they are equal. If a person loves himself less than he is, as for example the mind of man loves itself as much as the body of man must be loved, because the mind itself is more than the body, he sins and his love is not perfect. Likewise, if the mind loves itself more than it is, as if it loves itself as much as God must be loved, since it is incomparably less than God, thus it also sins exceedingly and does not have perfect love of self. However, he sins with greater perversity and injustice when he loves the body as much as God must be loved. Likewise, the knowledge is not perfect if it is less than that which is known and is able to be fully known. If it is greater, the nature which knows is greater than that which is known, just as the knowledge of the body is greater than the body itself, which is known by this knowledge. For knowledge is a specific life in the calculation of the person who knows. But the body is not life, and any life is greater than any body, not in mass but in force. Indeed, when the mind knows itself, its knowledge does not exceed it, but it knows itself and itself is known. Therefore when the mind knows its total self and not any other thing with itself, its knowledge is equal to it, because its knowledge is not from another nature when it knows itself. And when it perceives its total self and nothing more, its knowledge is neither less nor more. Therefore we rightly said that when these three are perfect they are consequently equal.

Also we are reminded at the same time, in whatever manner we are able to see it, that these—namely, knowledge and love—exist in the soul. They are, as it were, obscure when they are extricated; the result is that they are experienced and substantially enumerated, or, as I should say, essentially. They are not in the soul as if in a subject, as color or shape, or as any other quality or quantity are in the body. Whatever such a thing is, it does not exceed the subject in which it is. The color or shape of this body is not able to be the color or shape of another body. But the mind is able to love another thing besides itself with that love with which it loves itself. Likewise, the mind knows not only itself but also many other things. For this reason love and knowledge are not only in the mind as in a subject, but they are also there substantially, just as the mind itself, because even if they are mentioned as mutually relative, each is there in each one's own substance. They are not thus mentioned mutually as color and a relatively colored thing— since color in a colored subject does not have in itself its proper substance, because the colored body is the substance and the color is in the substance—but just as two friends also are two men which are substances, although they are mentioned not relatively as men but as friends relatively.

Likewise, although the person loving and knowing is a substance, knowledge is a substance, and love is a substance; but the person loving and the love, or the person knowing and the knowledge, are mentioned relatively in respect to themselves just as friends. Indeed, mind or spirit are not relative things, just as men are not relative. However, just as men who are friends are not able to be separated mutually from each other, so it is with the person loving and with love, or with the person knowing and with knowledge. Although friends also appear to be able to be separated in the body but not in the mind, insofar as they are friends, it can happen that a friend also begins to hate a friend, and on that very account would cease to be a friend while his friend does not know this and still loves. But if the love with which the mind loves itself would cease to be, at the same time the mind ceases to be loving. Likewise, if the knowledge with which the mind knows itself ceases to be, at the same time the mind will cease to know itself—just as if the head of anything with a head is certainly a head, and they are mentioned relatively to themselves, although they are also substances. For the head is a body and that which has a head, and if there is not a body neither will there be that which has a head. These are able to be separated mutually by a cutting; those are not able.

If there are some bodies that cannot be cleaved entirely and divided, unless they are composed of their own parts, they would not be bodies. Therefore it is said to be a part relative to the whole, because every part is a part of some whole, and a whole is a whole with all its parts. But since both the part and the whole is a body, they are mentioned not only relatively but also substantively. Therefore the mind is a whole, and its parts, as it were, are the love with which it loves itself and the knowledge with which it knows itself—and from these two parts the whole is composed. Or are there three equal parts with which the one whole is completed? But no part comprises the whole whose part it is. Indeed, when the mind knows itself as a whole, that is, knows perfectly, its knowledge is through the whole, and when it loves itself perfectly it loves itself as a whole and its love is through its whole. Therefore it is just as from wine, water, and honey one drink occurs, and each is through the whole and yet there are three (for there is no part of the drink, which does not have these three, for they are not joined as if water and oil but are entirely mixed and all are substances and the entire liquid is one specific substance, composed from the three), must some such thing be thought to be at the same time these three—mind, love, and knowledge? But water, wine, and honey are not of one substance, although it is from them by mixing that the substance of the drink occurs. However, I do not see in what manner those three are not of the same substance, since the mind itself loves itself and itself knows itself and also these three exist, so that not by any other thing is the mind loved or known. Therefore it is necessary that these three are of one and the same substance, and thus, if as by a mixing they were confused, in no manner would they be three, nor would they be able to be related mutually. For instance, if you would make three similar rings from one and the same gold, although joined to themselves, they are related mutually because they are similar, for everything is similar to some thing, and there is a trinity of rings and one gold. But if they should be mingled with themselves, and each is sprinkled through the whole of its mass, that trinity will perish and entirely will not be, and not only will it be mentioned as one gold, just as it was mentioned in those three rings, but it will not now be mentioned as three golden ones.

(5) But, when the mind knows itself and loves itself, a trinity remains in these three—mind, love and knowledge—and it is not confused with a mixture, although each is in itself and mutually the whole in the whole or each one in two or two in each, and thus all in all. The mind is also certainly in itself, because in respect to itself it is mentioned as mind, although in respect to its own knowledge it is relatively mentioned as knowing or having been known or knowable, and in respect to the love with which it loves itself, it would be referred to as loving, having been loved, or lovable. And knowledge, although referred to a mind knowing or having been known, in respect to itself is mentioned as known or knowing, for the knowledge with which the mind itself knows is hot unknown to itself. And love, although referred to the loving mind, whose love it is, in respect to itself is love, so that it is in itself because even love is loved, and it is not able to be loved, with anything except love that is, with itself. Thus these are each in themselves, but they are thus in one another, because the loving mind is also in love, and love is in the knowledge of the person loving and knowledge in the knowing mind. Thus each is in the two, because the mind which knows itself and loves is in its own love and knowledge, and the love of the mind loving and knowing itself is in the mind and its knowledge, and the knowledge of the mind knowing and loving itself is in the mind, and its love because it loves itself as knowing and knows itself loving. On account of this, the two are in each, because the mind which knows and loves itself is in love with its own knowledge and in the knowledge with its love, and love itself and knowledge are at the same time in the mind which loves and knows itself. We already have shown above that the whole is in the whole because the mind loves its whole self and knows its whole self and knows all its love and loves all its knowledge, when in respect to themselves these three are perfect. Thus in a wonderful way those three are inseparable from themselves. However, each one of them is a substance, and at the same time all are one substance or essence, although they are mentioned as mutually relative.

(6) But when the human mind knows itself and loves itself, it does not know and love something immutable. And in another way, each individual man, giving heed to what is active in himself, discloses his own mind by speaking. However, in another way he defines the human mind by special or general knowledge. Thus when a person speaks to me about his own mind, whether he understands or does not understand this or that, and whether he

wishes or does not wish this or that, I believe him; when he speaks the truth about the human mind specially or generally, I recognize and approve it. Thus it is obvious that what an individual sees in himself someone else may not see, believing what another person says to him. But what someone else is able to contemplate in the truth itself is another matter, the former is able to be changed through time, while the latter continues in its immutable eternity. For it is not by the seeing of many minds with the eyes of the body that we collect, through a likeness, a general or special knowledge of the human mind, but we contemplate the inviolable truth, from which, as perfectly as we are able, we should define not what sort the mind of each individual man is, but what sort it ought to be in eternal reasonings.

From here, when we rightly approve or disapprove of anything —by other rules remaining unchangeably beyond our minds—we are to approve among ourselves or disapprove specters of things of the body that are drawn through the sense of the body and in a certain way spread through the memory, and from which, these things, which have not been seen, are thought by means of a fictitious specter, whether it contradicts reality or accidentally is in agreement with it. For when I think of the walls of Carthage, which I have seen, and when I imagine the walls of Alexandria, which I have not seen, and when I prefer the same certain imaginary forms to some, I am preferring logically. The judgment of truth from above is vigorous and clear, and it is constant by the most unspoiled rules of its own right. It is covered as if by a certain cloud of images of the body. However, it is not enveloped and confounded.

But it is of importance whether I am under or in that darkness, as if I would be separated from the clear heaven, or just as it is accustomed to happen on the highest mountains whether during enjoyment of the free air I should observe both the brightest light above and the thickest cloud below. For where in me is the heat of brotherly love kindled when I hear that some man has endured more severe torments for the beauty and steadfastness of faith? If the man himself is indicated to me by a finger, I strive to join him to me, to make his acquaintance, to bind him in friendship. Thus if the opportunity is given, I come near, I address him, I exchange words, I describe my feeling toward him in which words I am able; and in turn I wish that this occurs in him and the same affection is described as mine, and by faith I engage in a spiritual embrace because I am not able so quickly to discern entirely the inner parts of his heart. Thus I love a faithful and strong man with a pure and real love. But if among our discourses he would confess to me or in some way incautiously disclose that he believes foolish things about God and seeks in him some carnal thing, and that he has endured those things in such an error or in the desire of hoped-for money or in useless desire of human praise, that love by which I was once borne to him is offended and, so to speak, rejected. Removed from the undeserving man, the love remains in this form from which I had loved him, believing him to be such a person—-unless, by chance, I now love him for this reason so that he should be such a person, although I had learned that he was not such. But in that man nothing has been changed. However, he can be changed, so that he may become what I believed he already was. In any case, in my mind the opinion itself has been changed which was in one way about him and now is in another. The same love has been turned from the effort of full enjoyment to the effort of consultation, since unchangeable justice from above orders me. Indeed, the form of unshaken and steadfast truth—in which I should enjoy the man, believing him to be good, and in which I consult that he should be good—this form fills with the same light of incorruptible and purest reasoning the look of my mind and that cloud of specter, which I discern from above, when I think of the same man whom I had seen, in an imperturbable eternity.

Likewise, when I bring to my mind, for example, a beautiful, perfectly rounded arch which I saw in Carthage, a certain thing, announced to my mind through the eyes and transferred to my memory, causes an appearance of images. But I perceived in my mind something according to which that work pleases me, where also if it displeased me I should correct it. Therefore we judge about these things according to that form, and we perceive that form by the contemplation of a logical mind. Indeed, we touch these present things with the sense of the body, or we remember images of absent things fixed in the memory, or we conceive such things from a likeness of them, which sort we ourselves would undertake by work, if we wished and were able. In one way we form in the mind images of bodies or see bodies through bodies. But in another way we seize principles and the ineffably beautiful art of such figures by simple understanding, because they are beyond the eye of the mind.

(7) Therefore with the sight of the mind we behold, in that eternal truth from which all temporal things have been made, the form according to which we are and according to which either in us or in bodies we work something with true and correct reason. And the truthful knowledge of things from there conceived we have among ourselves as a word, and we beget by speech within and it does not leave us at birth.

But when we speak to others, with the word remaining within we add the service of the voice or some other sign of the body, so that by a certain sensible remembrance some such thing also happens in the mind of the hearer which does not recede from the mind of the person speaking. Thus we do nothing through the members of the body in our deeds and words by which the manners of men is approved or disapproved which we do not anticipate by the word within brought forth among us. For no one willingly does something he has not said before in his own heart—which word is conceived in love, whether a word of the creature or of the Creator, that is, of a changeable nature or of an unchangeable truth.

(8) Therefore it is conceived by desire or love. Not that the creature must therefore not be loved, but if that love is referred to the Creator, it will not

be desire but love, for it is then desire when the creature is loved on account of itself. Then it does not aid the person using it, but it corrupts the person enjoying it. Therefore, because the creature is either equal to us or inferior, the inferior must be used for God and the equal must be enjoyed, but in God. Just as you ought to enjoy yourself not in yourself but in this One who made you, so also he whom you love as yourself must be enjoyed [Mark 12:31-33]. Therefore we should enjoy ourselves and our brothers in the Lord, and we should not dare to sink down from there to ourselves and, as it were, to slacken downward. The word is born when that which has been thought pleases, either for sinning or doing correctly. Therefore love, as a middle term, unites our word and mind from which it is begotten, and it binds itself with them as a third in an incorporeal embrace without any confusion.

(9) But the word conceived and born is the very same when the will rests in knowledge itself, which occurs in the love of spiritual things. For example, he who knows justice perfectly and loves it perfectly is now just, although there is no necessity of working outwardly in accord with it through the members of the body. However, in the love of carnal and temporal things, as in the progenies of animals, the conception of the word is one thing, the birth is another thing. In that matter, that which is conceived by desiring is born by attaining, because it does not avail greediness to know and love gold except that it also possess it; nor does it avail to know and to love eating or lying together, except that it also occurs; nor does it avail to know and love honors and powers, except that they appear. However, all that obtained does not avail: He said, "For he who will drink from this water will be thirsty again" [John 4:13], and therefore he also said in the Psalms, "He conceived sorrow and brought forth injustice" [Ps. 7:15]. He says that sorrow or labor is conceived when these things are conceived which it does not avail to know and to wish, and the mind burns and becomes ill with want until it attains them and, as it were, brings them forth. For this reason, *parta* [brought forth], *reperta* [discovery], and *comperta* [ascertained] are elegantly mentioned in the Latin language; these words sound as if they were derived from *partus* [birth], because "concupiscence, when it has conceived, brings forth sin" [James 1:15]. For this reason the Lord calls out, "Come to me all you who labor and are weighed down" [Matt. 11:28], and in another place, "Woe to you who are pregnant and nursing in those days" [Matt. 24:19]. And since he referred all things to the birth of the Word, things rightly done or sins, he said, "From the mouth you will be justified and from the mouth you will be condemned" [Matt. 12:37], wishing "mouth" to be understood not as this visible mouth but as within, invisible, of thought and heart.

(10) Therefore the issue whether all knowledge is a word or merely knowledge which is loved is correctly examined. We also know these things we hate, but those that displease us must be said to be neither conceived nor brought forth in the mind. Not all things which touch the mind in every way

are conceived so that they are only known, for these are not mentioned as words, as are those with which we are now concerned. Words which hold the spaces of times with syllables are mentioned in one way, whether they are pronounced or thought. In another way, everything known is mentioned as a word imprinted on the mind as long as it is able to be brought forth from memory and to be defined, although the thing itself displeases—in yet another way, when that which is conceived by the mind pleases. It is according to that kind of word that what the apostle says must be accepted: "No one says Lord Jesus, except in the Holy Spirit" [1 Cor. 12:3], although according to another conception of the word they say this, concerning whom the Lord himself says, "Not everyone who says to me, 'Lord, Lord,' will enter into the kingdom of heaven" [Matt. 7:21].

Nevertheless, when those things which we hate, correctly displease, and correctly are disapproved of, the disapproval of them is approved, pleases, and is a word. The knowledge of faults does not displease, but the faults themselves do. It pleases me that I know and define what is intemperance, and this is its word. Just as in art there are known faults and their knowledge is correctly approved when an authority distinguishes the species and deprivation of excellence, so to assent and to deny either that it is or that it is not, yet it is worthy of blame to be deprived of excellence and to abandon in a fault. It belongs to the art of morals to define intemperance and to state its word, but to be an intemperate person belongs to that which is reproached by that art of morals—just as to know and to define what a solecism is pertains to the an of speaking (but to do this is a fault which is reproved by the same art). Therefore the word which we now wish to distinguish and to get to know thoroughly is knowledge with love. Thus, when a mind knows and loves itself, its word is united to it by love. And because it loves knowledge and knows love, then the word is in love and love in the word, and both are in the person loving and speaking. But every knowledge according to the species is similar to this thing which it knows. For there is another knowledge according to privation which we speak when we disapprove. This disapproval of privation praises the species and thus is approved.

(11) Therefore the mind has some similarity to the known species, whether this pleases or its privation displeases. Therefore, as far as we know God, we are like God, but we are not like him to the point of equality because we do not know him so far as he himself knows himself. And just as when through the sense of the body we learn of bodies, a certain likeness of them occurs in our mind which is a specter of memory. (For bodies are not at all in the mind when we think of them but their likeness, so we err when we approve of the likenesses for them, for the approval of one thing for another is an error. However, the imagination of the body in the mind is better than that species of the body, inasfar as this is in a better nature, that is, in a vital substance, just as the mind is.) Thus when we know God, although we are made better than

we were before we knew, and especially when this knowledge, pleasing and worthily loved, is a word and that knowledge becomes a likeness of God, yet it is inferior because it is in an inferior nature. Indeed, the mind is a creature but God is Creator. From this it is inferred, when the mind knows itself and thus approves, that the same knowledge is its word so that it is entirely equal to it, equal and identical because it is not the knowledge of an inferior essence as of a body or of a higher one as God. And since knowledge has a likeness to this thing which it knows, namely, this of which it is the knowledge, this has a perfect and equal likeness inasmuch as the mind itself, which knows, is known. Therefore knowledge is both the image and the word because it is expressed about that mind while it is equal to it by knowing, and because that which is begotten is equal to the person begetting.

(12) Therefore, what is love? Will it not be an image, will it not be a word, will it not be begotten? Why does the mind beget its knowledge when it knows itself, and does not beget its love when it loves itself? If the reason for its knowing is that it is knowable, the cause of its love is also because it is lovable. Thus it is difficult to say why it has not begotten both. This questioning concerning the greatest Trinity itself, the most powerful Creator God, to whose image man has been made, ought to move men whom the truth of God invites to faith through human speech to inquire why the Holy Spirit is not believed or understood to be begotten by God the Father so that he himself is also mentioned as Son.

We are now attempting to investigate this question in the human mind, so that when the inferior image, as it were questioned by us, with which our nature is more familiar, answers we may guide a better exercised keenness of the mind from the illuminated creature to the unchangeable light. However, truth has prevailed; just as no Christian doubts that the Son is the Word of God, so the Holy Spirit is love. Therefore let us return, for a more accurate questioning and reflection concerning this thing, to that image which the creature is, to the rational mind, where there is a knowledge existing temporally of some things, which was not before, and a love of some things which were not loved before. This knowledge and love expose to us more distinctly what we should say, because it is easier to explain things, which are comprehended in the order of the times, to the speech itself, which must be temporally directed.

Thus first let it be obvious that something can be knowable, that is, is able to be known and, however, may be unknown. But it cannot happen that that should be known which is not knowable. Clearly from this it must be held that everything, whatever we know, begets in us knowledge of itself, for knowledge is brought forth from both, from the person who knows and that which is known. Thus, when the mind itself knows itself, it alone is the parent of its own knowledge, for it itself is that which is known and the one who knows. It itself was knowable even before it knew itself, but its knowledge was not in it when it itself had not known itself. Therefore, because it knows itself it begets a knowledge of itself equal to itself, because it does not know itself to be less than it is; nor is its knowledge of another essence, not only because it itself knows but also because it knows itself, as we mentioned above.

Therefore, what must be said about love? Why does it not appear, also when the mind loves itself, that it has also begotten the love of self? For it was lovable to itself even before it loved itself, because it was able to love itself, just as it was knowable to itself even before it knew itself, because it was able to know itself. If it were not knowable to itself, never would it have been able to know itself. Thus if it were not lovable to itself, never would it have been able to love itself. Thus, why should it not be said that it has begotten its love by loving, just as by knowing itself it has begotten its own knowledge? Or, then, does it obviously show that this is the principle of love from which it proceeds? Indeed, it proceeds from the mind itself, which is lovable to itself before it loves itself, and thus is the principle of its own love by which it loves itself. But, therefore, is it incorrectly stated that it is begotten by the mind—as is knowledge of itself by which it knows itself—because it has already been discovered by knowledge, which is described as brought forth or discovered, because the inquiry, which will come to rest, often precedes this goal? An inquiry is a longing for finding out, which means the same as if you would say "discovering." But those things which are discovered are brought forth, as it were, wherefore they are similar to progenies. Where are they from except knowledge itself? For, articulated there, as it were, they are shaped. Although the things we find out by seeking already existed, nevertheless knowledge which we reckon as a progeny born did not exist. In addition, that longing which exists in seeking proceeds from the person seeking and in some manner is suspended; and it does not rest in that goal where it is directed unless that which is sought has been found and joined to the person seeking. Although that longing for—that is, inquiry—does not appear to be love by which that which is known is loved (for knowing is still in process), nevertheless, it is something of the same kind. Already it is able to be mentioned as will, because everyone who seeks it wishes to find it, and if that which is sought pertains to knowledge, everyone who seeks wishes to know. But if impassionately and immediately he wishes it, he is said to study which phrase ought to be used especially in the obtainings and attainings of certain teachings. Therefore a certain longing-for precedes a bringing forth in the mind, by which by seeking and finding out what we wish to know, a progeny, knowledge itself, is born. On this account, that longing-for by which knowledge is conceived and brought forth is not able correctly to be called birth and progeny. And the same longing-for, by which is longed for the knowing of a thing, becomes love of the thing known while it holds and embraces the pleasing progeny—that is, knowledge—and unites it to the person begetting. And there is a certain image of the Trinity: the mind itself and its knowledge, that is, its progeny and its word concerning itself, and love. These three are one and one substance. And the progeny is not less while the mind knows itself so much as it is; nor is love less, while the mind loves itself as much as it knows and as much as it is.

Bibliography

Anatolios, Khaled. *Athanasius*. London: Routledge, 2004.

Ayres, Lewis. *Augustine and the Trinity*. Cambridge: Cambridge University Press, 2010.

_____. *Nicaea and Its Legacy: An Approach to Fourth-Century Trinitarian Theology*. Oxford: Oxford University Press, 2004.

Beeley, Christopher A. *Gregory of Nazianzus on the Trinity and the Knowledge of God*. Oxford: Oxford University Press, 2008.

Behr, John. *Formation of Christian Theology*, vol. 1: *The Way to Nicaea*. Crestwood: St. Vladimir's Press, 2001.

_____. *Formation of Christian Theology*, vol. 2: *The Nicene Faith*. Crestwood: St. Vladimir's Press, 2004.

Bright, William., ed. *The Orations of Saint Athanasius against the Arians*. Oxford: Clarendon Press, 1873.

Cunliffe-Jones, H. and Drewery, B., eds. *A History of Christian Doctrine*. Edinburgh: T&T Clark, 1978 and Philadelphia: Fortress Press, 1980.

Grant, Robert. *The Early Christian Doctrine of God*. Charlottesville, VA: University of Virginia Press, 1966.

Gregg, Robert and Groh, Dennis. *Early Arianism – A View of Salvation*. Philadelphia: Fortress Press, 1981.

Gwatkin, H.M. *Studies of Arianism*. 2nd rev. ed. London: Bell, 1900.

Jonkers, Engbert, ed. *Acta et Symbola Conciliorum Quae Saeculo Quarto Habita Sunt*. Textus Minores 19. Leiden: E.J. Brill, 1974.

Kelly, J.N.D. *Early Christian Doctrines*, 5th rev. ed. London: A. & C. Black, 1977 and New York: Harper and Row, 1978.

Laird, Martin. *Gregory of Nyssa and the Grasp of Faith: Union, Knowledge, and Divine Presence*. Oxford: Oxford University Press, 2004.

Lietzmann, Hans. *The Founding of the Church Universal*. Vol. 2 of *A History of the Early Church*. Translated by B. Woolf. 2nd rev. ed. London: Lutterworth Press, 1949.

_____. *From Constantine to Julian*. Vol. 3 of *A History of the Early Church*. Translated by B. Woolf. 2d rev. ed. London: Lutterworth Press, 1950.

Luibhéid, Colm. *Eusebius of Caesarea and the Arian Crisis*. Galway: Irish Academic Press, 1981.

Mason, Arthur, ed. *The Five Theological Orations of Gregory of Nazianzus*. Cambridge Patristic Texts 1. Cambridge: University of Cambridge Press, 1899.

Mountain, William and Glorie, F., eds. *S. Augustini De Trinitate. Corpus Christianorum*, Series Latine, Vol. 50. Turnhout, 1967.

Mueller, Fridericus, ed. *Opera Dogmatica Minora*. Gregorii Nysseni Opera 3/1. Edited by W. Jaeger. Leiden: E.J. Brill, 1955.

Newman, John Henry Cardinal. *The Arians of the Fourth Century*. 3d rev. ed. London: Longmans, Green & Co., 1871.

Opitz, Hans Georg, ed. *Urkunden zur Geschichte des arianischen Streites*. Vol. 3/1 of *Athanasius Werke*. Berlin and Leipzig, 1934-35.

Pelikan, Jaroslav. *The Christian Tradition*, vol 1: *The Emergence of the Catholic Tradition*. Chicago: University of Chicago Press, 1971.

_____. *Credo: Historical and Theological Guide to Creeds and Confessions of Faith in the Christian Tradition*. New Haven: Yale University Press, 2003.

Prestige, George L. *Fathers and Heretics*. London: S.P.C.K., 1963.

_____. God in Patristic Thought. 2d rev. ed. London: S.P.C.K., 1952.

Rawlinson, A., ed. *Essays on the Trinity and the Incarnation*. New York: Longmans, Green & Co., 1928.

Stead, Christopher. *Divine Substance*. Oxford: Clarendon Press, 1977.

Wiles, Maurice. *The Making of Christian Doctrine*. Cambridge: Cambridge University Press, 1967.

_____. *Archetypal Heresy: Arianism Through the Centuries*. Oxford: Oxford University Press, 1996.

Williams, Daniel H. *Ambrose of Milan and the End of the Arian-Nicene Conflicts*. Oxford: Oxford University Press, 1995.

Williams, Rowan. *Arius: Heresy and Tradition*. 2d. rev. ed. Grand Rapids, MI: Eerdmans, 2001.

Young, Frances M. *The Making of the Creeds*. London: SCM and Philadelphia: Trinity Press, 1991.

_____.with Andrew Teal, eds. *From Nicaea to Chalcedon*. 2nd ed. Grand Rapids, MI: Baker, 2010.

Key Themes

Arianism – the belief, traceable to the teachings of the Alexandrian presbyter Arius in the 4th century, that Christ was a creature and therefore not coeternal with God the Father.

Begetting – in what became orthodox Christology, refers to the process by which the Son eternally proceeds from the Father in a way that preserves (against Arianism) the coeternality of the Son with the Father. "Begetting" is thus distinct from "making" or "creating," both of which imply the subordinate status of the thing created.

Dynamic Monarchianism – also known as adoptionism; the belief (later deemed heretical) that Christ was a mere human upon whom the Spirit descended. Dynamic Monarchianism thus denies that Christ is coeternal and of one being with God the Father.

Economy – in Trinitarian theology, "economy" was used by Irenaeus and others to refer to the ordered process of God's self-disclosure within salvation history (as narrated by scripture). In other words, it is the Trinity as experienced by humanity. The "economy" of the Trinity within history is, for most patristic theologians, distinct but not fundamentally separate from the processions of the persons of the Trinity within the intrinsic being of God.

Logos – in Greek philosophy, the principle of reason that animates both human rationality and the fundamental order of the cosmos. Logos-Christologies worked to integrate this Greek philosophical tradition with the references to Christ as the "logos" in Christian scripture, particularly in the gospel of John.

Modalist Monarchianism – the teaching that there is one Godhead which can be designated indifferently as either Father or Son within salvation history. God thus is understood as a monad with no fundamental distinctions or persons (*hypostases*) within God's being. This style of Trinitarian thinking was eventually rejected as heretical by the council of Nicea (325 c.e.) and Constantinople (381 c.e.).

Monotheism – the belief, common to Christianity and Judaism (and later Islam), that God is fundamentally "one" in being. Throughout the Trinitarian controversy, theologians – both those declared orthodox and those later deemed heretical by the ecumenical councils- worked to describe the economy of the Trinitarian persons (Father, Son, and Holy Spirit) while maintaining the fundamental monotheism (oneness) of God.

Ousia – "substance" or "being." Debates throughout the Trinitarian controversy ranged as to whether the Son, as second person of the Trinity, is *homoousios* ("the same substance") as the Father, or *homoiousios* ("of like substance") as the Father, or entirely subordinate to the Father (as in Arianism). At the council of Constantinople in 381, agreements between the *homoousios* and *homoiousios* parties led to the definition of orthodox Trinitarianism as the belief that God exists as three *hypostases* (persons) and one *ousia* (being).

Procession – the principle of motion within the Trinity. "Procession" refers to the means by which the Son is eternally begotten by the Father and the Spirit is sent eternally from the Father and (in the West) from the Son.

Subordinationism – a general label for any Trinitarian theology that suggests that the Son and/or the Spirit is subordinate to God the Father. Arianism, with its suggestion that the Son is not coeternal with the Father, is a form of subordinationism.